Traveler,
Your footsteps are the path
and nothing more;
Path maker, there is no path.
You make the path by walking.
By walking, you make the path.
ANTONIO MACHADO

Pay attention. Be astonished. Tell about it.
MARY OLIVER

No one can build you the bridge on which you,
and you alone, must cross the river of life.
NIETZSCHE

INTRODUCTION

Poet, artist, traveler, mother, mentor, businesswoman, friend, confidant, student, grandmother, activist, author, great grandmother. At 84, Martha Talburt is the matriarch of our large family. And although she moves more slowly through the world after a stroke on her 80th birthday, her vitality and creativity would be impressive for someone half her age. With 6 children, 18 grandchildren and 3 great grandchildren, Martha stays connected to everyone in her impressive family flock. Birthdays, anniversaries, and other milestones are always remembered with a poem, or a work of art posted to a Facebook account.

It's hard to find many silver linings that resulted from our collective struggles with the Covid pandemic. Fortunately for our family, 2 years of isolation from each other and friends was the most severe consequence of the pandemic. Virtual happy hours and Zoom family gatherings were a small comfort but a woefully inadequate substitute for the real deal.

This introduction is dedicated to a master of silver linings. An irrepressible beacon of positivity who has profoundly impacted my outlook on life and has served as one of my most influential teachers. During the 2 years of isolation, Martha used that time to create this extraordinary book. She spent hundreds of hours combing through a lifetime of sketch books and journals to curate the opus.

Thanks Mom for this gift. Thank you for filling these pages with such wisdom, wit, and positive energy. You've given me, our family and hopefully many others, an inspiring testimony of a wonderful life.

STEPHEN CANNON

INVITATION FROM GOD

Get over yourself — take a day or a week
To get over yourself — make the leap.
Get over yourself, girl, and give Me a hand
(I'm beckoning you; this is not a command)
Get over yourself. Hear the deep inner call.
Remember, my dear, you're a bridge not a wall.

Before I check out, I want to share this life, take you along on a ride through it — the vehicles being my poetry, journal essays and artwork, all of which have helped me immeasurably to make it through. This is a compilation of poems, artwork, and journals — how I've processed my stuff through the years. I've been in many a dark place and when there, drawing, writing a poem or journal entry has built a ladder up and out of the pit of the moment. Just the act of writing about what hurts, what sucks, gets the attendant feelings out into the air, and not left simmering within. But it's certainly not all about hurts — the wonder, hilarity, joy, and delight are even more important.

In telling my story, it helps to remember the me of back then in the third person, so I'll be toggling between "I" and "she" throughout these pages. The past is never really past and the "now of back then" comes clearer when I think about the me of back then as she.

Some years ago, I wrote a cluster of recollections of my childhood summers, spent in a small seaside community on the Connecticut side of Long Island Sound called Indian Cove. It's stunning to me now, re-reading these memories, reflecting on my good fortune to have had such idyllic summers.

Back When

A HORN REMEMBERED

My father was old enough to be my grandfather when I was born. I cannot remember him with hair or real teeth — not that he looked old and toothless. Far from it. He had, in fact, excellent dentures. But to blow the horn and call us home he had to remove them.

"Us" consisted of five children, a large brood for those days. I was the youngest. Only the Haskell's in our neighborhood equaled us in number — and they weren't even Catholic. Daddy was interested in giving good things to his family, good things as he perceived it. He approved of summers on the water, and in 1942 purchased a cottage in Indian Cove, Connecticut, a quaint, non-pretentious resort on the Long Island Sound. I loved the water, at three swam like a fish, and spent countless days submerged, to the point of stumbling home with lungs so moist every breath brought a cough.

My summers were lively, wet and wonderful clear up to chubby pre-adolescence, at which point I recognized boredom and noisily succumbed to it. Endless hours of water play, sand creations, crabbing, peanut butter sandwich picnics in the woods, fishing and climbing the rocks were replaced by hanging around with my gang at Bishop's Store. This was a mom-and-pop shop across from the mudflats at the mouth of the cove. It had a soda fountain, provisions, and Mr. and Mrs. Bishop offered a welcome refuge for groups of different aged kids. My parents couldn't for the life of them understand why we spent so much time cooped up in that dark place instead of being outside in the sunshine.

What they did understand, however, and expected us to as well, was when Daddy blew the horn, we were to return home. Home was a barn red bungalow with white trim on the high side of Indian Cove, about a half mile walk uphill from The Store. Perched on a knoll, a wide screened porch girdled two sides and commanded a lovely view of the Sound, Faulkner's Island, boats, rocks, and Mulberry Point across the bay. On the porch was an odd assortment of furniture — my mother was no decorator. My favorite piece was a rocker for two which my mother's father, a carpenter, had built. For me this was a loveseat in the truest sense. I remember rocking in it with my grandfather — we called him Pipay. He'd tell me jokes, in a thick, French accent and would rate them. "Dis one is wort a nickel .... dis one only two cents." I would inhale his woody, pipe-tobacco smells, roar at his silly stories and mostly luxuriate in his attentiveness when no one else seemed to pay me much mind.

My father loved a good buy and the cottage fit the bill — as did the foghorn, a galvanized tin instrument with a worn wooden mouthpiece he got from a boat captain in Guilford. One good blow carried for miles. No family had anything like it; we kids were mortified. The horn bleated and the entire cove knew my father was rounding up his family. More embarrassing yet was the sight of him doing the calling. Not a tall man, five-eight at most, he had a large barrel chest, and spindly legs, both features greatly accentuated when he was relaxing around the cottage in baggy shorts and an old tee shirt. A salesman by nature and profession, Father was a self-confident man. He planted himself like a rooster on the highest porch step, spit dentures into one hand, lifted horn to mouth and blasted off — blap, blap-blap-blap, blap-blap, cheeks exploding, face purple. My father loved this horn.

One day I'd had quite enough of the ignominious paging system. No more than twelve at the time, but well along on my descent into adolescence, I heard the sound from clear down at the store and chose to ignore it. I can't remember I was having much fun but do recall with clarity the fierceness of my determination — perhaps just to see what would happen, testing new waters having abandoned the old. The horn brayed with increasing urgency every five minutes for the next forty-five when finally, my stand collapsed in a whimper, and I headed home in terror to face my maker. This part I don't remember at all, but Mrs. Cameron, the nosey lady next door, later reported the following to my parents: "Miss Martha, chin forward, striding like Bette Davis down the driveway, was muttering loudly, 'Behold, I enter this house in fear and trembling!'"

Mutiny ended, punishment meted: I was porched for at least two weeks, read and sighed a lot, experienced even deeper waves of adolescent ennui, and survived the consequences to spend many more summers at Indian Cove — summers beautiful and boring, safe and constricting. Father wanted it that way, all of us secure and within easy reach. He's dead many years now, as is my mother. My own children are grown, and I am an old woman, remembering the tinny sound of summer and my father, teeth in hand, calling his children home.

GRANDMA LITTLE DAY

She sat on the screened-in porch of her daughter's bungalow in Indian Cove, about two houses down from my backyard. I went often to visit her. Grandma Little was the oldest person I had ever seen. Her hair, wispy white like a cloud, was swept up in an old-fashioned bun and framed a patrician face etched with wrinkles. A pink shawl rested on her shoulders as she leaned forward in her wheelchair to better catch the light. Long knobby fingers had minds of their own, as they expertly worked knitting needles, producing yet another of the countless washcloths Grandma gave to all who came calling. Made with snowy white cotton yarn, the pattern was simple. She taught me and I did fine with the knitting stitches, even learned to purl, but the crocheted scalloping around the edge presented problems. My pudgy little fingers could never successfully wield the crochet hook.

But Grandma Little was patient and gracious. I was never turned away from her door — would spend hours in her company. She made me feel good about myself and, unlike at my house, always seemed interested in what I had to say. I'd knock knock on the screen door and Mrs. Weaver, Grandma's daughter — who was plenty old herself — would let me in with a smile. Sometimes I'd show off new reading skills. Other times we'd work on our knitting. And sometimes I'd just be there with Grandma, not talking at all, a difficult feat for me generally but not with her — she smelled good, too, like lavender.

One summer my mother was voted president of the Indian Cove Improvement Association. I was a precocious seven-year-old at the time and thrilled with a title which I felt added considerably to our family cache, puffing continually to my friends, and finally having to be shut up with a scolding. The Association decided to have a party in honor of Grandma Little –now a beloved icon in the community. It would be held on the lawn in front of the Weaver's cottage with Grandma on the porch having front row vantage. One of the older Cove boys was enlisted to play accordion, a potluck picnic was planned, children were to come in costumes, and prizes would be awarded for the cleverest outfits. Grandma Little Day was to be the event of the season.

Tragedy intervened. Racing down the hill in a new red wagon, I went out of control trying to turn the thing and fell out, causing a compound fracture of my right elbow. Aunt Dee was taking care of us. A nurse, she must have been horrified when they brought me home, arm bleeding and hanging off me at an odd angle. She wrapped it in newspaper and raced me to the emergency room in New Haven, about an hour's drive. They clamped a scary black ether mask over my face, and I awoke with a huge cast on my arm. I spent one night in the hospital in a room with a little girl named Cookie whose mother had tied her to their toilet and abandoned her. I overheard nurses telling the story which fascinated and terrified me — a weird distraction from my own misery. I was given Jello and ice cream and the next day taken back to Indian Cove a hero.

Then came an awful time — no swimming — torture for the child who was used to spending entire days in the water. But plans for Grandma Little Day had progressed. Dishes for the potluck dinner had been assigned, they booked a drummer in addition to the accordionist, and the whole Cove was buzzing. I, the newly self-appointed neighborhood tragedienne, was consumed with anxiety about what to go as and how to get that prize for best.

Walt Garrity, an old family friend who'd been in my father's World War I division, also had a summer house at the Cove. As the event was scheduled for shortly after July 4th, he suggested I be the Spirit of '76. With one arm already cast and slung, they'd only to wrap me in a few more bandages, bind my head with gauze, bloody the whole affair up with ketchup and fashion me a crutch for my one good arm. The grownups were roaring with laughter as they sketched out this terrific idea and I went along with the whole thing, delighted to be center of attention and wondering what on earth was a Spirit of '76.

My older sister, Jane, was around eleven that summer. She and her friends were going as the ace, king, queen and jack of hearts. The four girls, bottoms up on the porch of our cottage, spent hours designing, cutting cardboard, and finally painting their masterworks, which they wore like sandwich boards on the day of the party.

Roberta Walker and her little sister, Susan, who was my age, went as a pack of Winston cigarettes and book of matches. Cigarettes were advertised heavily on television in those days and a cigarette box and matches, dancing to "Winstons taste good like a cigarette should" were featured in a national commercial. The Walkers created perfect replicas which they wore over their heads, seeing through tiny peep holes in the lettering. Only their legs showed, decked in shiny white boots to the knee.

The parade formed at Dew Drop Inn, a silver-weathered old house just up from the beach. The drummer and accordion player led the march with Yankee Doodle Went to Town and all Indian Cove lined up on the sides of the road applauding as we wound our way up the same hill of my recent disaster to present ourselves in front of the Weaver's screen porch, where Grandma Little sat serenely in spite of all the fuss. The weather was perfect, and the children sashayed about in their finery, having more fun than Halloween, in the middle of the summer. Mr. Garrity, a portly man with an abundant mop of gray hair, well messed up for the occasion, dressed as a clown tramp in clam digger trousers tied with a rope and huge bare feet he'd made out of brown paper stuffed with cotton. Prizes were awarded. I, having affected an excellent limp to go along with my attire, won a first prize. So did Roberta and Susan Walker, but I was sure their mother and father had made their outfits and that wasn't fair because my sister's face card gang had done everything all by themselves and they came in second!

Grandma Little viewed many more festivals in her honor. We got news of her death one winter when my other life was being lived in town. Childhood for me was segmented into the days we were away from the Cove, went to school and had responsibilities, and summer days when we roamed free and had fun times like Grandma Little Day. I was twelve or thirteen, had emerged from chubby childhood into shapely, awkward adolescence and was old enough, my mother thought, to attend the wake. Flattered and terrified by such a vote of confidence in my maturity, I wore stockings for the first time ever, a belted maroon hand-me-down suit and black suede shoes with two-inch heels borrowed from my sister. Thus, dressed in yet another costume to honor the old lady, I approached her open coffin with a mixture of pride in my appearance and abject fear of what I was about to see. As it turned out, Grandma Little dead was as sweet and pretty as she'd been alive. I was stirred by this waxen image of my friend, white hair contouring her elegant old face which appeared as content in death as it had in life.

My attendance at Grandma Little's wake helped bring closure to a child who'd been excluded from funeral activities when both grandmother and then beloved grandfather had died. The thinking was that a young child would be damaged by exposure to the rituals of death. No one recognized how much more negative was the effect of leaving the child out, alone, and bereft. Now, however, I was once again welcomed and found comfort at Grandma Little's door.

HYMN SING

Softly and tenderly Jesus is calling...

the melody rests on warm evening air. About forty folks cluster on rocks skirting the beach, singing words from moldy old Methodist hymnals carried down in a box. The sun casts purple and mauve shadows on the rock bank leading from Indian Cove round the bend to Sachem's Head. We gather for Hymn Sing every Sunday evening during my many summers in this small resort community on the Connecticut side of Long Island Sound.

Reverend Teitjen directs. Tall and bald, he leans crane-like toward his beachside congregation, one hand flails a yellow pencil baton, the other rests on the portable organ two men haul from Mrs. Sperry's house on the hill, down the road and onto the sand. Mrs. Sperry is a plump matron with hennaed hair swept up atop her head. She holds court proudly on the organ — her legs pump the pedals energetically to keep air flowing into the instrument; her springy curls bounce merrily in time to accompaniment more enthusiastic than proficient.

Musical prowess or lack of it, however, is not what earned Mrs. Sperry her permanent place in my family lore. The story goes that after my parents returned from their first European trip, she queried my mother with a sniff, "And Ev, did they understand *your* French in Paris?" Now those were fighting words, for my mother had studied years to transform the French-Canadian French of her upbringing into a more classical European dialect. Self-taught and fiercely proud, Evie's response to such condescension did us all proud. "Did they understand *your* English in London?"

Our weekly hymn singers represented every denomination — a rare gathering in days when all thought the other folks were heading straight for hell if they weren't of our specific religious persuasion. Being Catholic, most of the fun for me was the in the lusty singing of these "protestant" songs, none of which I'd ever heard in my more pallid church rituals. I'd curl up delightedly next to my father's gravelly baritone rolling out Holy, Holy Holy. Another favorite was:

> *Let the lower light keep shining. Send a beam across the wave.*
> *Some poor fainting, struggling seaman you may rescue, you may save.*

I was hooked — waist-deep in water, holding high my lantern for some half-drowned sailor to flop gasping onto the beach. *O Mary conceived without sin* simply could not compete.

The song fest ended each week with a teen-age soprano giving us a fluty version of the Lord's Prayer. Sometimes it was my big sister, Ducky (a nickname for Anne which she wisely dropped when away at college,) who'd had a leading role in her high school's Pirates of Penzance production. She was a star! Sometimes Roberta Walker sang, her youthful beauty and solemn sweetness forgave any flaws in pitch or projection. Awestruck, I dreamt of the day when I could shine up there between Mrs. Sperry and the good reverend, mesmerizing one and all with my own inspired rendition.

Just a scent of saltwater can bring me back to the rock perch by my father, basking in rare closeness to a man who raised his five children with detachment which mystified, leaving us all scrambling as adults to conjure up our own ego strength.

He'd been a front-line medic and ambulance driver in World War I, had witnessed and mopped up after countless savage battles, pieced together limbs, ministered to soldiers whose lungs were ravaged by searing gas. My father came out of that war intact physically but hid in the back of his sock drawer the many medals he'd earned. One was the Silver Star. His children only learned of this hero's trove after he died and was buried with full military honors.

I relax my father's confusing grip when I remember Hymn Sings in small, artless Indian Cove where I grew up ... Reverend Teitjen stoops toward his little flock, pencil swooping in time to Mrs. Sperry's thumping chords. *Day is dying in the West* ... Father's deep, wobbly voice resonates in the evening air...*Heav'n is touching earth with rest* ... My off-key piping drowns out our side of the choir while my older, newly adolescent sister, Janc, head averted, hunches down on her rock. ... *Wait and worship while the night* ... Mother's voice, strong and well enunciated, arcs toward the organ. ... *Sets her evening lamps alight through all the sky.* The rosy wash of sunset splashes beach and rocks as night approaches.

MORNING WALK IN INDIAN COVE

Awash in wafts
of honeysuckle,
sprinkle of skunk
keeps me grounded.
Salty air cleanses the senses
while robins, sparrows and catbirds
chip the way.
Morning light splashes
white boats in the tiny bay.
At the horizon floats Faulkner's Island,
benevolent gray whale
between sea and sky.
Swallows flit and swoop;
a coven of gulls convenes on the rock bank.
Mockingbirds flash stripes.
Doves coo. Waves lap.
My heart rocks in the rhythm.

CLIMBING THE ROCKS CIRCA 2002

(WITH THANKS TO ROBERT FROST)

Whose rocks these are I think I know
I used to climb them long ago —
My tiny tread then sure and fleet
I tried again this morning, though,

And quickly learned that time, the cheat,
Had wiped that knowledge from my feet —
Left just a memory in my heart
Of skills I'd had but can't repeat.

I left my bench, made a fine start,
When halfway to the beach — not smart —
I leapt a crevice in the rocks
Fell and tore my shin apart.

Thus, with blood dripping in my socks
I hauled myself back up those rocks
Whose banks were slippery and steep
With promises I could not keep
Limped to my house and went to sleep.

IF JINGLE SHELLS

If jingle shells
Were legal tender
I'd prescribe a spending bender —
Buying bird songs, scents of flowers,
Quiet hours in salty air
With morning mist —
A billionaire philanthropist
Is what I'd be,
My bank a beach
Beside the sea.

CACOPHONY

Those mourning doves
have set my teeth
on edge this morning.
I want to scream,
girls! End
the threnody!
Listen to wrens,
cardinals, finches,
even the sparrows
get it. But you
and your oooo
oooo, oooo's,
no matter how sweet
and seductive
the rhythm.
I want to scream
girls! Your sighs
     will get you
     nowhere.

Soul Space

A twenty-something year old woman sits in lotus position in a small, antique Quaker meeting house. It's mid-winter in Ridgewood, NJ. She's wearing a long, gray plaid wool cape, with black braided rope belting the front, which provides her a private tent of sorts. The room is only partly filled, and it is silent prayer time, the congregants all listening intently for "that of God." The woman's husband is in another place — St. Elizabeth's Roman Catholic church in the next town, where he has ushered their six small children ahead of him in a front pew. He sits guard at the aisle.

Oh, she loved that cape — that woman who was me, searching so early in her young adulthood for soul space — quiet space, seldom experienced and frequently longed for in her tumultuous young life as mother of six children under nine. To not go to Mass on Sunday was not only frowned upon in the Catholic church, but it was also labeled grievous sin and that young woman did not even imagine how radically intrepid were her actions. She was simply following survival instincts, regardless of her husband's judgment and disapproval, or the church's.

I can still call to mind the musty scent of the tiny old building, its beamed ceiling swept up into a peak, filled with quiet loving energy — no sermons, no thou shalt nots, just a much-needed loving space for my soul.

MULTI-TASKING

MEMORIES OF A MOTHER OF SIX

I chuckle to think about
when I was young
the myriad tasks
I could get done.
Simultaneously,
it seemed, I was able
to nurse a new baby
set the table
mop a floor
launder clothes
and more —
God knows —
dinners and snacks
by constant demand of the pack
growing 'round me.
So where,
you may ask, is that new baby now?
With four of her own
and another with nine,
eighteen grand kids and counting!
My bountiful children
are breeding like Mom —
which is why they keep asking
about multi-tasking.

HOUSEWIFE'S LAMENT — CIRCA 1970

(WITH APOLOGIES TO WM. SHAKESPEARE)

What foul stench from yon hamper doth emanate?
Alas! Must it be forever mine the loathsome task
Of withdrawing the contents therein?
Examining pockets for hidden crayons
Whose dark nectar, on contact with the dryer's heat
Could be released and spill itself, unkindly,
On the newly clean apparel.

Yea, it is mine and alone mine
The daily attack on grit and grime.
And, too, the ceaseless move of yonder mop and rag.
Could I have known t'would be such a drag!
And hourly sibling quibbles to be soothed and smoothed
E'er larger conflicts be the consequence.
Could I but get me hence! Flee from this place
For merely an hour. Yea, then could I face
The endless demands on my patience and grace.

Tis useless, Lady. Heed no more this futile rhyme.
There's to be no escape. Thy destiny is sealed.
Breakfast's plates must be scrubbed.
Sup's potatoes need be peeled.
So get thee to thy labors, Madam. Cease this idle dreaming.
Yon carpet lies with dust befouled,
Thy precious babes are screaming.

To flee or not to flee is not the question.
But to remain and midst the turmoil acquire not indigestion
Of the mental sort so common to my lot.
Yea, must I stay and query not.
Ours is not to wonder why —
Ours is just to do — and sigh.

The Now of Back Then

You may need a magnifying glass for this — it's so full of life!

"My fortune, my children" was my grandfather's often-repeated mantra, with which I heartily agree — but this is undoubtedly the most challenging bit of my collection of memories and reflections: the twenty-five-year arc of child-raising years and the six small lives for which I was responsible. Kerry, the oldest, arrived when I was twenty-one; Julie, the youngest, when I'd just turned twenty-nine. How do I adequately pull representative stories from that sweep of years, describe the fun and delight, the terror and dismay and celebrate "my fortune" — those lives now grown and flown from my tiny nest.

A picture helps — and this one's a doozy! Sarah created the collage for a project in middle school about her family. She got an A. Her photo collage to this day remains a memory aid / jolt / meditation a la famiglia.

Sarah was the first female child to grace our family — a wonder and very special blessing after four boys. Julie arrived less than three years later to add more feminine energy into the mix. My cup ran over — Kerry, Stephen, Mark, John, Sarah and Julie — my fortune was made!

I was so young — we all grew up together during the sixties and seventies. Laughingly, I picture myself in the now of back then — nursing a baby, pushing a broom with my foot, and reading a book — multi-tasking! Kerry enjoyed a mere thirteen months of being kingpin, when Stephen joined the nest. The two became inseparable — a bond which remains to this day. Mark created a triad — fourteen months after Stephen — and John arrived seventeen months later — born the day after President John Kennedy was assassinated.

> She, hugely pregnant, wearing a bright blue plaid maternity jumper, walks slowly to the back of Miller's Pharmacy in Wyckoff, NJ. The entire town, it seemed, was steeped in silent shock — except for the three bumptious boys, toddlers all, who were noisily skipping and bouncing around her. At the pharmacist's counter, she solemnly asks for a bottle of castor oil. The pleasant lady gazes at her and down at her condition and starts to smile — then chuckle a bit. She, the hugely pregnant one, startled out of her solemnity, smiles back then bursts out in a laugh they both share and silently agree that it is simply impossible to bear another day of being nine months pregnant and have to go through the awfulness of a presidential assassination and what was to follow it. She paid for the castor oil, gathered her little boys, piled them into the back seat of the car (no car seats in those days — seat belts either — a wonder we all survived) and drove the short distance to her friend's house — who also had a pack of little boys — where the children played together and the friend mixed her a smoothie of orange juice, a little vodka, and the castor oil. Baby John was born the next morning.

Now we were a family of six, but not for long. Exactly fourteen months later, the arrival of my first girl was a blessing beyond blessing. Sarah jokes that I kept a ruffled hat on her for the first few years. Poor kid — I constantly decked her out in bonnets, straw hats with bows, and smocked pinafores. Three years later, Julie came into the picture. It was my joy at Christmastime to outfit these precious girls in matched red velvet dresses. But following four brothers, the dresses soon morphed into jeans and sneakers and all the rough play clothes required to compete in that busy, boy-dominated mix. To my pride and delight, Sarah and Julie were more than up to the task, Sarah in grade school won the President's Physical Fitness Award several years in a row. None of the boys matched that. She was full of determination and grit, characteristics which remain, as today she smoothly runs a large, successful restaurant and catering business.

Julie took to the soccer field with a will to win that perfectly matched the competitive spirit of the household back then — and now, as much as ever, on the golf course. The boys played football, wrestled, and skied, and all the children rode bikes everywhere. One Easter, when Dad had gotten a bonus, we bought six shiny new bicycles and hid them around the yard, each with an Easter basket hanging from its handle. Dribbles of grass and jellybeans led the way to each hiding place.

Then, there was the Easter which had Mark, our artist, hanging up a large poster he had made — a colorful hot air balloon floating across the sky with CHIST HAS RISEN emblazoned across the basket. Spelling was never his forte.

Children's lives were freer in those days. Summer brought long days of not having to get up early, of running in packs with the neighborhood kids, coming home breathless to grab a sandwich for lunch and heading back out again. When we put an in-ground pool in the backyard, it became the neighborhood swimming hole and hot summer days echoed with the sounds of a dozen or more children playing Marko Polo. Our Mark, the family character, with innumerable interests, one being magic, was around twelve when he gathered a crowd of kids to watch him perform a Houdini trick, lock himself up in chains, and drop into the deep end of the pool, sink to the bottom, somehow release himself to come splashing up like a dolphin, a great smile from ear to ear.

Stephen was a friend magnet — still is. Kids gravitated to him, forging friendships which remain to this day. Always intellectually curious, he was an excellent student, loved school, and would often come home and discuss things he'd learned. I'll never forget one cold winter evening, the eight of us were lounging around a cozy fire in the living room, being regaled by Stephen reading aloud the Nun's Tale by Chaucer, which was particularly bawdy, replete with descriptions of farts and kissing bare behinds. We were left helpless in tears, howling with laughter as he put particular emphasis on the bawdiest bits.

Laughter helped. The things I mostly remember involved hilarity. Like the Friday evening Kerry, who was a high school freshman or sophomore, was home and somehow it was just the two of us watching a popular TV comedy show. One skit involved a puppeteer with his hands stuck up two plucked, headless chickens wearing bow ties — fat roasters like the many I bought for family dinners — and making them sing and dance. Kerry is by far the funniest member of our family — has the quirkiest sense of humor and still leaves us in stitches much of the time. The naked, dancing chickens hit us both in the same funny bone. We shared this bond of huge laughter which I consider a peak experience — right up there with Maslow's best.

Reading to the children was an event for which I always had warm and fuzzy hopes which, alas, were seldom delivered. The pushing and crowding around me to see the pictures and non-stop complaints of one or another that they couldn't hear, or one of the boys pinched or pushed another out of the way. Always a notable exception, however, was my Christmas Eve reading of The Little Match Girl, when they all waited breathlessly for me to cry as she huddled in the icy corner and lit her last match, the angels gathering round her. Much to their satisfaction, I never failed to deliver — and still fill up with tears reading the story.

There were accidents aplenty, trips to the emergency room, breaks, burns and sprains. (I used to joke about writing my memoir, with one chapter being entitled "Aspirin, Ice and Elevation".) John, at four, was hit by a car — sirens, crowds gathered, ambulance trip to hospital, heart stopping fear — He miraculously survived with only a minor concussion and scrapes and bruises all over his little body — no broken bones. He spent a night in the hospital under observation and came home a hero the next morning. We carried him out of the car and into a crowd of neighborhood children gathered round, pressing him with bags of penny candy from the nearby store. Kerry had spinal meningitis, Sarah's legs were seriously burned, and she had to undergo a painful healing process. Julie's little legs were turned in and as a toddler had to wear what we called her "nite nite shoes", which were separated by a metal bar to help straighten her legs. Kerry and Stephen would carry her upside down by the bar while she laughed and loved both the attention and the ride.

Laughs and tears, teen-aged fights aplenty, serious one-on-one conversations at Friendly's, when a child needed to discuss an issue privately. Hot fudge sundaes or massive ice cream cones helped. But so much, from my current perch in Elderhood(y), is a blur as the time has flown by.

Unforgettable, however, was the major family holiday of these years — a cross-country trip to Montana, driving in a twelve passenger Ford Explorer Wagon — in 1976, before SUVs got their name. The front seats were two captain's chairs which swiveled, between which rested a large cooler we packed with sandwiches, snacks, sodas and goodies for the day. We drove from around 9AM to 3PM and stayed nights in Ramada Inns (with swimming pools.) Daily, new wonders were presented to our eastern sensibilities — Ogalala, Nebraska, the endless plains of Kansas, winding over and through the Rocky Mountains, Grand Teton, Wyoming and a lake surrounded by mountains, vistas to take your breath away — then on into Gallatin Gateway, Montana, where we spent ten days at The Nine Quarter Circle Ranch. We had our own cabin; a fire was set for us each day. Guests were served meals in a large main cabin, family style. No money was exchanged. It was all on the American plan. Divine.

More divine was the big sky country — we easterners had never seen such glorious expanses of space: impossible blue skies dotted with cotton clouds, mountains and forested valleys, plains sparkling with wildflowers. We knew nothing about horses or riding them. But the children and Dad took to all this like naturals. Guests were ranked by ability and age — the older boys in one, Sarah and John in another, and Julie, eight at the time, was in a special group for younger kids. And then there was me, the wimp, who quickly decided I didn't take kindly to horses or riding — particularly on the first day, when my horse turned around and bit me in the boot. So I spent my days with guitar, journal, art supplies, and a good book in hand — wandering by myself, settling down to simply BE in one or another magnificent site, basking in tincture of time *and* space for my soul.

One day, as I walked by the younger group's paddock, Julie came running up to me, breathless with excitement — *"Mama, a horse blew a blue bubble from her bottom and a baby horse was in it!!"* This was truly a wondrous adventure for each one of us.

We attended our first rodeo ever in Bozeman, Montana, when one of the riders, a rather plump woman, riding in a perfectly aligned march of horses, kept breaking rank by slipping off her mount and struggling to get back on. It was a comedy ruse, of course, but so well done that we were all hysterical, stomachs in pain from laughing — yet another Maslow peak experience.

We left Kerry at the ranch — he was hired as a dishwasher and, at age sixteen, we felt it would be a good experience for him. It was. Six weeks later we picked him up at Newark Airport, in a well-worn red ski vest, hair nearly to shoulders, toothpick in mouth, and responding with laconic "howdies" and "yups" for the next month or so.

The long drive east was challenging. A northerly route back home took us through the Badlands of South Dakota. But the children were tired, cranky and missing home and their friends. The inside of the car seemed smaller as the vast expanse of landscapes whizzed by. We made it in one piece, however, and the nearly three-week adventure became an important cornerstone of my family's childhood. Each of the children has returned, with their own families to the ranch and had an equally magical experience.

Today I ponder how on earth I was able to manage this monumental task of child-raising — the greatest accomplishment of my life. My children, surrounded by their own children, ask the same and I can only answer I don't know. But the I don't know is filled with wonder, gratitude, and a sense, as suggested by the Spanish poet, Antonio Machado, on the first page of this book: we make (made, will make) the path by walking.

Another family collage is appropriate here — and as blessedly full of life as the first. Once again, I must ask you to do a forward leap with me — from the now of back then to the now of now, where I am as I write this. You may need that magnifying glass for this one, too.

... And while I'm at it, here is a quite recent poem that I think fits here:

THE PEBBLE OF ME

A pebble
Dropped in a pond
Is me.
The first ripple out
Is my family
Which, as it grows,
The ripples flow free —
Further away
From the pebble of me.
This is, I see,
As it should be

Breakage

A WOMAN'S TALE

There once was a woman whose tale I'll relate
She lived in an egg with her family of eight
All sugary frosted that ovum domain
Could be viewed from outside through a glass windowpane.
Inside, even sweeter it was than the shell
Those sunny inhabitants living so well
That onlookers envied the warmth of the scene
Where the father was king and the woman his queen.

She ruled her egg dwelling with color and grace
Her clever hands reached every inch of the place:
Paintings hung on the walls, soup simmered on the burner,
A fire glowed and buds blossomed — such efforts earned her
Devotion, affection, approval, applause —
On which she thrived greatly, the lady, because
In the egg life she'd chosen those pay-offs were key.
Every once in a while, though, she yearned to be free

From the egg and its king and the children and home
And giving and caring, "but to go on my own,"
She would whine, "I'm unable."
Now comes a turn in this ovular fable.
I'll tell you, but first there are pertinent facts
Concerning those sugar walls under which cracks
Had for years been appearing that the icing had hidden.
To examine the damage was strictly forbidden

By egg law which stated: "When surface is sweet
Avoid what lies under it." Now, I repeat
The aforementioned turn, which occurred in the spring,
The egg throne collapsed and sent sprawling that King.
The crash of the throne and the man who sat on it
Sent shock waves through the egg to degrees cacophonic.
The sugary plaster fell off in great heaps
Exposing the fissures and weakness beneath;

So too did the scales fall from off the Queen's eyes
Who soon understood more had caused the demise
Of her eggy abode which kings, horses and men
Could never by now put together again.
The woman concluded her days would be nicer
Away from that shell and her role as its icer.
This tale has a moral, you've heard it from me:
Egg life is not all that it's cracked up to be.

A WIFE'S TALE

Little Marty housed a Hearty Laugh and Merry Grin
who together kept her fresh and undisturbed by sin.
Faithfully they stood their guard beside the shadowed door —
keep the darkness out, they'd shriek, give us light
and more sunshine, we can never get enough.
Cheerfully they blocked that other Unappealing Stuff.

But one day erupted when Stuff crashed in and broke the door,
clobbered Hearty with a stick, knocked Merry to the floor —
roughshod did that Stuff ride o'er her tidy little nest
Marty looked in horror at the god-forsaken mess.
"Dearie me, what shall I do to straighten up the place?"
"Nothing", Stuff replied, "be still and know that I am grace."

FOUR POSTER, 1958

Discovered moldy
in an antique dealer's shop
we buy you on the spot,
apply hours of sublimated passion
to your shine and set you up grandly
on the driveway that summer we were engaged.
My father is impressed
by the weight of your sideboards.
A married sister insists
we'll never make a better purchase.
My mother thinks it premature. Uncle Arthur,
 the engineer, finds you well constructed.

As do we. Your cherry patina blushes
in the light of early marital fumbling,
stoically endured.
We reward your patience
with six fat babies.
And now children climb, bounce,
test your solidity.
Your graceful finials — swung on,
teethed on, nose-picked on —
survive the indignities
and take a proud polish. Better than I.

Sleepless vigils ensue
as grinding adolescence, too, we oversee.
Rigid sentinels, we await the errant homecomings,
denouements at the turn of the lock,
and tedious explanations
at the foot of the bed.
Friend, I salute you
even as, the marriage long over,
you lie somewhere dismantled
and molding once more.

TALE OF A VIRGIN MOTHER

A middle-aged virgin mother of six
came out of her house to try some new tricks.
For twenty-five years she'd been cloistered inside
attending her duties with housewifely pride.
But now from that nest she'd been untimely thrust
into a world she knew not. And thus
with viscerals burbling that warm Summer day
she stepped out on a stage, not knowing the play.

The first scene was pleasant, the setting benign —
with a widower named Walter she went out to dine.
A gentleman, he wore a tie stitched with whales
and they both dabbed their eyes while exchanging sad tales.
When the evening was over they shook hands goodnight.
She proffered a grip that was firm — it seemed right
to convey her affection yet not go too far.
Not bad, she mused later. *I felt like a star!*

Next she drove north to a poets' convention
her writing, she reasoned, required some attention.
Daydreaming while driving: *Delights there await me,*
Maybe even a sensitive poet to mate me.
O readers, our lady, so sheltered, naïve,
saw things at that conference she couldn't believe
and those poets — those writers she'd thought so aesthete —
were writhing offstage in a market of meat.
During the day, to be sure, they gave many a lecture
but evenings, well, I'll let your own mind conjecture.

The middle aged virgin and untrained performer
was shocked by a play in which no one had warned her
about the scenes on-going backstage
with professors and artists unseemly engaged.
So, ignoring the sideshow and masking her fright,
she attended by day and stayed in at night,
averting the moves for which this meet was known.

A little bit wiser she headed back home,
concluding ... *My poems have not yet found their soul*
but the prodigal mother is not my best role.
Thus, she returned in the manner she'd come —
a middle-aged virgin still. END OF ACT I.

ACT TWO

She's walking east on 86th Street, tears streaming down her face, muttering to herself, "I'm nobody's Dulcinea." In the thick of typical New York crowds, no one gives her a second glance.

She has moved there at the perfectly awful end of her 27-year marriage. New York was the ideal place, where she could be anonymous and ponder on the crosstown bus at 4 o'clock on a Friday why it is that everyone is holding hands and seem to continue doing same through the weekend. But, being nobody's Dulcinea, she doesn't get to. She's lonely and sad a lot of the time — it shows on her face, and no one notices or cares.

But the days are far from all bad/sad/mad downers — there are hilarious highlights, like meeting up with her kids at a restaurant/bar called CRONIES and drinking wine, swapping stories and munching on the best fried zucchini sticks in town; then walking home, stopping for the light at 86th and 1st and watching a man stomping his feet and loudly declaring, "FUCK, FUCK, FUCK!" because he'd missed the light and had to wait. Oh, there's nothing like the street entertainment in New York City!

> And there, in liminal space — the space of sitting with our truths;
> the place of mystery, the unknown — we acknowledge our feelings —
> the power and depth of each one — giving them space to roll through us,
> to breathe and take on life.
>
> FELICIA MURRELL

I have spent a good deal of time in liminal states. The threshold period between endings and beginnings is often a waiting time, a time to reflect on what's gone before, as well as the choices for what lies ahead, choices that are both exhilarating and terrifying. It is a time of big dreams and bigger doubts.

During these times my journals have been invaluable repositories, into which I would pour doubts and fears, dreams and goals, feelings of confidence and despair, all of which became grist for the poetry mill. I worked out a lot of stuff through my poems. I could be in a desperately awful state of mind, miserable and frightened, and the creative act of writing, of crafting a poem, lifted me out of that dark place.

TIDES I

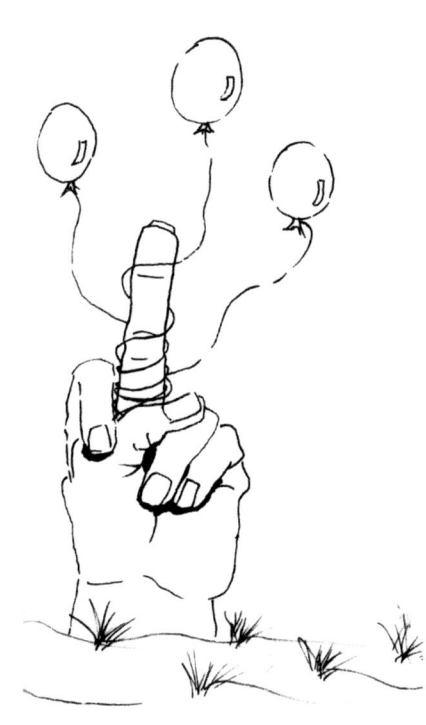

I'm not a pipsqueak by the sea,
those gulls are shrieking lies to me.
The tide is out, I'll grant that much,
with dead fish, beer cans, crabs and such
washed on my shore
but I know more
awaits me out beyond that crest.
I'll climb the wave before I rest
and let it carry me to land
where I'll make new prints in the sand.
I'm strong. I float. I'm my own boat.
So I'll ignore the taunting words
of stupid, garbage-eating birds.

TIDES II

I am a pipsqueak by the sea,
those gulls are speaking truth to me.
The tide is in and rising fast,
I'm holding on but cannot last
much longer as each wave descends
and spits me out upon the sand.
I'm weakened — sunk —
a floundering junk —
who can't ignore prophetic words
from graceful, soaring water birds.

WAVE OF FEAR

The week before last I felt weak and downcast
Unmoored, so to speak, from my tether
Neither fish neither fowl, I mused with a scowl
And continued quite under the weather

What's this all about, I worried and doubted
I'd ever get out of the squall
Alone and at sea, what will happen to me
I shivered and started to bawl.

Then a great wave arose to engulf, I supposed,
My poor little boat and me in it
But to my surprise when I looked in its eyes
The wave winked and said *dive in and swim it!*

So dive in I did, just as the wave bid me
The going was rough for awhile
I spluttered and choked then tried a few strokes
On my own, the wave watched with a smile

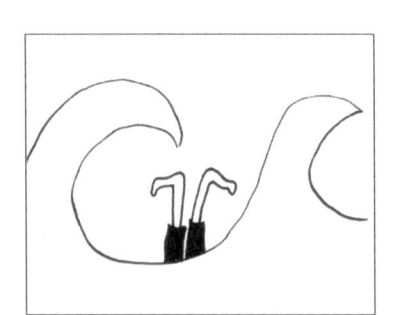

Well, before I could say S.O.S or May Day
I found myself riding that swell
There wasn't much to it.
  I learned to slide through it.
    I'm doing it now.
      Can't you tell?

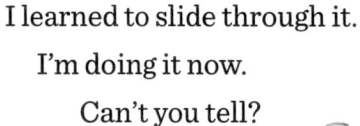

This brings me to another story:

She is on the phone, wiping her eyes, blotting her nose, speaking to her son, who has called from Germany. *"Mom, can't you just say FIDO ?"*

FIDO is a favorite West Point expletive, Mark explained in the phone call to the her that was me after I had bent his ear for ten minutes, weeping over my inadequacy as an advertising sales rep, struggling with my new job in New York city, taking every perceived rejection personally, and trying desperately to grow thick skin. It means: FUCK IT AND DRIVE ON!!

Mark was stationed in Germany at the time, serving his five years, post West Point, as a Lieutenant in the Army. He would call often and was a masterful yay-sayer, coach and encourager during what was a challenging transition time.

Mom — you took six kids and sold us all on values, a good work ethic, and how to be unselfish and kind — you are a salesman, and I was your best customer!! You just gotta keep saying FUCK IT AND DRIVE ON to yourself!

... and I have, dearest Mark. The sheer vulgarity of it and the memory of your enthusiastic tutelage during those early years of creeping up a formidable learning curve, never fails to lift me up and amuse me out of whatever doldrum I might be weathering.

I lasted in the world of business for ten years, selling advertising space for two national trade publications. It was terrifying, adventurous, tedious, exhilarating work — how on earth am I going to convince this guy that he needs a four-color, full-page ad in my magazine?? I was surrounded by supremely confident young yuppies the age of my kids, who acted like they knew everything. I was anything but self-confident, muttering FIDO to myself, taking frequent rest room breaks to have a cry, then apply eyedrops of Murine and head back out to the phones for yet another self-defined "rejection", when yet another prospect didn't want what I was offering. *You gotta grow thick skin, girly,* advised one old pro of a salesman.

And then there were the business lunches and being hit on and acting the naive innocent, as if I didn't get the double entendre or the subtle invitation. Being the mother of six helped, a fact that I kept very much in evidence in my light patter across the table, sharing funny, interesting (to me) stories.

And I learned that being the mother of six, having for years run that "factory called home", having catered non-stop to the needs of everyone in my family — making them all look good — had been extraordinarily effective preparation. I was well schooled in meeting the other person's needs, which is what selling is all about!! I sold more ad pages than the gang of yuppies combined.

WHAT TO DO WITH MY LIFE

(A LIST)

Roll
Bend
Spin
Sway

Crash
Creep
Cry
Pray

Hoot Holler
Howl Roar
Puzzle a lot
Ponder more

Giggle Guffaw
Grimace Grin
Pull in gut
Stick out chin

Grab it
Shake it
Love it
Give it

Mostly
do my best
to live it.

HOW TO

THANK YOU, GERTRUDE STEIN

How to
Sort through
Life's do?
Don't.
Can't do.
Life's yarn
Skein twine.
Unwind?
Can't un-
Do line.
Won't do
Undo.
Don't whine.
In time
How don't
How do.
In time
End rhyme.

Questing

OUTWARD BOUND

In November 1986, less than six months in New York and still job-hunting, I decided to spend Thanksgiving week in Southwest Texas, whitewater canoeing down the Rio Grand on an Outward Bound adventure, specially designed for people in transition. I was one of the oldest, having just turned 47, a hothouse flower with no experience whatsoever in the wild. But that's the point. By spending time in totally unfamiliar environments in nature, you reach down deep into wellsprings of strength you never knew were there — strength I sorely needed in this transition.

JOURNAL ENTRIES — OUTWARD BOUND — NOVEMBER 22-29, 1986

SOLO: The sun has gone down behind the canyon now. There's daylight left, but it has gotten chillier, so the long underwear is now on — plus dry chinos, a long-sleeved shirt, and dry socks and running shoes. I'm ready for nighttime — sweaters in abeyance, sleeping bag ready and cozy on a soft patch of dry ground. I'm sitting by the Rio Grande, which is flowing quickly about twelve feet below me — no sounds but the river's whoosh and gurgle, an occasional bird warble and a rustle of breeze in the shrubs. A massive rock wall faces me — I'll probably be climbing one like it tomorrow, after this solo … it's darker now and I've climbed into my sleeping bag, resting against a rock. I feel like I'm in a cosmic theatre and the curtain's about to open. Two hawks have been soaring above me for ten minutes effortlessly taking the air currents — a metaphor — God — let me use the currents in my life with the hawks' grace — less wing flapping — more soaring.

I'm glad for this flashlight — gladder for the millions of stars. Now I'm watching two satellites move slowly across the sky and then dazzling shooting stars which arc so quickly that I almost miss them. This is better than watching a fire or the ocean. I imagine myself as having been in this same place centuries ago, seeing the same sky. I have a feeling the only disappointment about this solo will be its brevity.

WHITEWATER: I'm front rower in a two-person canoe — behind, my partner is screaming, "pry!! Lean to port!" Water whooshes round the boat — there's a huge rock on the right just ahead. I lean left and plunge my paddle out and toward the boat, moving it sideways, which pulls us into a "tongue" (water driveway) and away from the rock. We're both terrified.

The screaming woman was a young doctor from Texas who was as inexperienced as I, but driven by perfectionism, which came to a head on the third day of our partnership, after a particularly challenging run. Upon making it back to the riverbank, without tipping over or getting dumped, I said to her, "We did a great job!" which I felt we really had. She snappishly replied that we hadn't done it right - that she hadn't done it right. Well, mature me lost it at that point. I started to cry, shouting at her "You're just like my husband was — never satisfied — nothing's good enough for you!" Later, around the nightly fire, we iron out our differences — sort of — with the help of the whole group.

ROCKCLIMB: I'm hanging by my crotch, dangling in the air from a belaying harness, 40 feet above the ground, halfway up an 80-foot rock wall, sobbing. "Let go!" they're calling from the top — "Re-group, look around and find another foothold." I take a deep breath, reach toward another chink and grab hold, pulling closer to the wall, where I find a foothold, dig in and haul myself up another six inches. Finally, I make it to the top, climb over the lip of the cliff and fall — sobbing once more — into the arms of the wildly cheering group.

Of all the Outward Bounders that day, my rock climb was surely one of the slowest and certainly the most frighteningly emotional experience of the whole week. But I did it.

Later, rappelling down that same cliff was a pleasure. The big takeaway here was discerning between objective and subjective fear. Objectively, I was perfectly safe, the belaying system tried and true. But subjectively — of course — I was scared to death! And the whole point is to push through the emotional barrier!

THE ODYSSEY OF THE LITTLE RED HEN

Back in the city a week after Outward Bound, I'm uptown walking north on Lexington Avenue and see a storefront window blaring — ADVENTURE TRAVEL. I go in and am greeted by a friendly, young red-headed woman named Sandy, and say to her, "I want to make a journey." Sandy jumps into action and provides me with an armload of brochures and literature.

The idea for a journey was born on my flight back to NY from the Outward Bound in Texas. I decided I liked adventure. Sandy and I soon became good friends (I've always loved redheads) and trip planning partners. I came in off the street and gave her probably the best assignment in her young career as a travel agent. For weeks we cobbled together an itinerary. I would travel west around the world — first stop, Tahiti. I took to calling my journey THE ODYSSEY OF THE LITTLE RED HEN, "The Little Red Hen," being another favorite of my childhood books, whose words throughout the book, — *"I'll do it myself!"* became my clarion call.

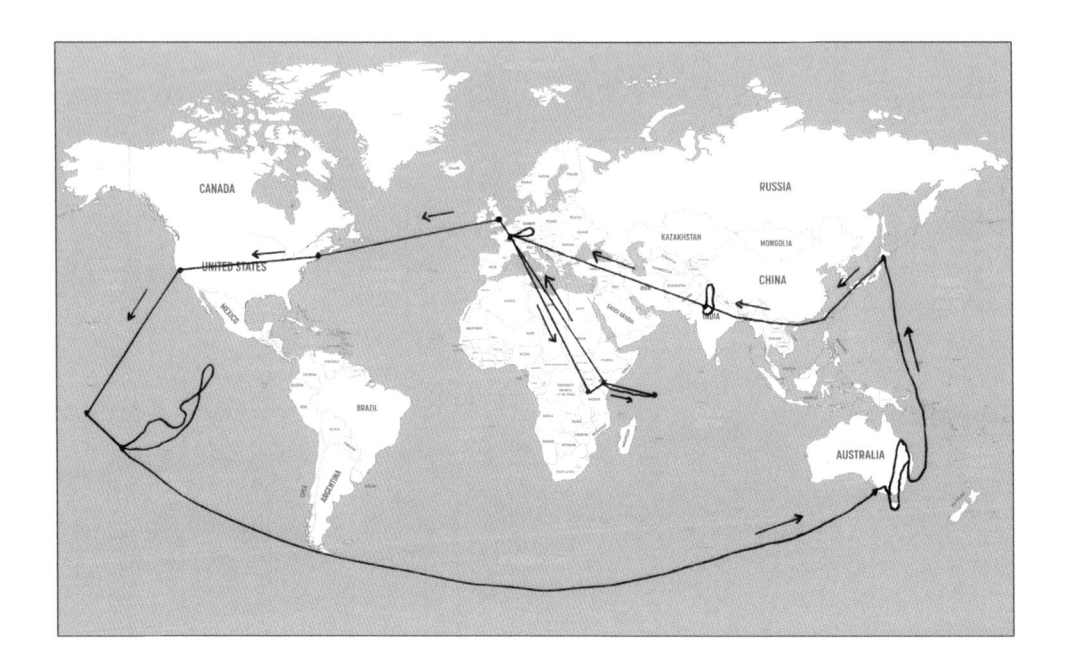

MARCH 4, 1987 — DEPART

West to San Francisco to Tahiti to Easter Island to a small ship expedition which visited the South Pacific islands — including a day on Pitcairn to meet ancestors of Mutiny on the Bounty sailors — back to Tahiti and a few days rest on the island of Moorea across the bay. From there two weeks in Australia, bushwhacking in the Blue Mountains — bicycling across Tasmania — sailing and camping in Whitsunday Islands in Northern Australia — city stays in Melbourne and Sydney. Sydney to Tokyo, Japan — city stay then tour of Japanese tea houses in Japanese Alps — Buddhist monastery stay in Kyoto — Osaka and flight to Hong Kong. City stay then flight to New Delhi, India. City stay then flight to Srinigar in Himalayas and house boat stay on Lake Dal. (No tourism anymore in this region due to Indian-Pakistan conflicts.) Delhi then Jaipur then Agra and Taj Mahal then flight to Veranasi — Mouth of Mother Gangii River. City stay in Varanasi — also known as Benares. Flight to Kathmandu in Nepal. City stay. Back to India and flight to Paris. Paris stay — then overnight train to Karlsruhe, Germany and family reunion and Mark and Carmen's wedding. 10 day road trip with Julie through Germany and Austria and Northern Italy — Milan. Back to Germany — Julie flies home — I train from Karlsruhe to Amsterdam. City stay in Amsterdam. Flight from Holland to Arusha, Africa. Pick up a hiking group and 5 day climb up Mt Kilimanjaro. Made it to top. Rest in Arusha after climb. Taxi from Arusha to Kenya border. Taxi from Kenya border to Nairobi. City stay in Nairobi. Bush safari in Kenya. Back to Nairobi. Fly to Seychelle Islands for several days r&r. Stayed in a thatched hut on stilts on beach. Seychelle Islands back to Nairobi. Nairobi to London. Meet Joyce at airport. City stay then travel by car 14 days through SW England, staying in pubs and b&bs, Dartmoor and Exmore — followed path of Druids and visited many prehistoric sites — stones and such — Stonehenge, etc. City stay in Bath. Back to London overnight. Fly home — London to New York

AUGUST 24, 1987 — ARRIVE NYC

EASTER ISLAND, THE SOUTH PACIFIC

I'm jogging on a dirt path along the coast of Easter Island (Rapa Nui), on the other side of the world, five days into my journey. To my left, huge tumbles of lava rock, glistening with sea spray, comprise the coastline. I'm wearing my running shorts — which make me feel like an athlete. I've recovered from jet lag and think I can take on anything the world has to show me. The sky is impossibly blue, the South Pacific an equally impossible turquoise. A salty breeze is in my face as I listen to a running tape the children made up for me — *The World is Calling*. I can't believe I've pulled it off.

SRINIGAR, THE KASHMIR, INDIA

India was the height and nadir of my six-month world journey. I spent two weeks there, traveling alone. A major takeaway: never travel alone in India — the both/and of it is jarring, shocking, unsettling — and so awesomely beautiful, and stunningly fascinating, you need a traveling partner to help assimilate and talk through the emotional impact of all you're seeing and experiencing. Here are some clips from my journals and memories.

JOURNAL ENTRY — MAY 25, 1987 6 A.M., ON THE HOUSEBOAT CRYSTAL PALACE ON LAKE DAL, SRINIGAR — IN THE KASHMIR — NORTHERN INDIA

"Wonderful Flowerman" has just skimmed by, in his shell boat (called a shikara) loaded with flowers. He's heading for market. Out about fifty yards two more shikaras, loaded with kohlrabi and other vegetables, are heading in the same direction to the morning farmers market. There's a riot of noise — birds shrieking, roosters crowing raucously, in counter-point — the sound of chanting drifting across the lake — men at prayer. It's Ramadan and 80% of the people here are Muslim. The lake is up a about 4-5 feet due to flooding in the last weeks and the entire spring planting will have to be redone. Farmers grow mostly vegetables here — planted in floating gardens built from weeds found in the Dal and and woven together into floating mats that form the base of the gardens. A little later, I'm sitting comfortably on a flower printed cushioned bench, more like an armchair, in the center of a shikara, being paddled to the morning vegetable market as the sun is rising over the Himalayas which surround the lake. The boat seems tiny and fragile, a petal on the lake. But the oarsman sits confidently in the stern, dipping his heart-shaped paddle into the glassy water. I'm looking over at the amazing houseboat about fifty yards away on which I've been staying for two days — my hotel accommodations on Lake Dal. Everything is bathed in the golden light of dawn, as am I.

RIDE FROM JAIPUR TO AGRA

My poem gasps in heat and dust.
Its words melt in sweat
and hold their breath
to withstand smells.
Bougainvillea blossoms riotously
in magenta and orange
beside mud huts.
Ladies, too, blossom along the road
in chartreuse, scarlet and cerise saris,
walking slowly with waterpots on heads —
or bending in nearby fields
scraping grass into piles for fodder.
Oxen, goats, camels and dogs
compete with cars, trucks, buses,
bicycles and people.
A bearded leper waves bandaged stumps at passersby —
grasps alms between snaggled teeth.
A white humped cow serenely creates mayhem
Chewing her cud in the center lane
My poem shields its eyes in the glare
Rubs them to ease the strain.

THE TAJ MAHAL, AGRA, INDIA

I'm wearing my favorite t-shirt — the one with the world emblazoned on the front. It's lightweight white cotton, as is the peasant skirt — both loose and cool, a necessity in the 100 degrees + weather. I walk up a long pathway by a reflecting pool, which leads to the arched entrance into the Taj Mahal. I'm one of hundreds of tourists, all Indians, celebrating one of their many annual festivals. Women are wearing brightly colored sequined saris, which sparkle in glittering counterpoint to the white mica-speckled tiles of the building. To say I am awestruck would be an understatement — dumbstruck — thunderstruck — also inadequate. A profoundly beautiful monument built to honor love. The whole atmosphere glows. How is it I get to be here, in this place, in my up to now quite limited life???

MT KILIMANJARO, TANZANIA, AFRICA

JOURNAL ENTRY — JULY 6, 1987, 6 P.M.

I'm sitting on the porch of the Mandara Hut at 9,000 feet, having poley, poley (slowly, slowly) completed day one of the climb. I composed the poem enroute: It's a lovely help composing poetry — busies the mind and keeps a rhythm in your head — kind of like some poems I've written while running. I'll try to add to this each day. I seem to have anthropomorphized my walking stick — imbued it with life and energy — masculine energy. It will serve nicely as the "man in my life" for the next 5 days.

JULY 7

Enroute today we see baboons and smaller monkeys playing in the trees. Our walk takes us through a tropical rain forest — great swags of moss garlanding the trees, the air so thick with moisture you could drink it — and varied smells of the flora — now sweet, now pungent. Smells too of the porters, a body odor so strong that staying upwind proves a better ploy. Bird twitter accompanies our walk — and walk is the operative word. Amble, almost, is what we do. Slowly slowly is the rule of thumb (foot) to let the body accommodate gently to the thinning air. At this altitude I'm having no problem at all but am mainly concentrating on establishing a slow and easy rhythm 1-2-3-4-5-6-7-8 — like my running pace. The Jesus prayer mantra speaks itself continually behind my face, alternating with the counting. And with my staff I'm one minute Moses parting the sea, the next minute Morgan of Avalon with her magic wand. I think I'll need both images for the days ahead.

I

My walking stick and I
Fitting partners
In this attempt to ascend
Kilimanjaro.
Long phallic thing
I grab your shaft smartly
Plant your metal tip
In the dirt ahead
And pull from you
The masculine energy
I need for the climb.
I can do it I can do it
I can do it I can do it
And you nod and sway in time
To my silent chant
We'll dance together
For the next few days
And set a proper rhythm
To marry this mountain.

JULY 8

At 12,300 feet now — a 7 and ½ hour walk from Mandara to Horombo Hut. A rhythm established itself in my slow stride — a slow rhythm — a very long day. We started out at 8:20, arrived here at 4:20 with a ½ hour stop for lunch. The day consisted of putting one foot in front of the other for what seemed an eternity. Tedious but my mind set is — I'm committed to this enterprise and walking poley poley is the game plan. There's a hint of headache playing around my forehead — more of a pressure — but I feel okay and more determined than ever to make it the whole way. I took today gently. At times, with the sun shining on the moors, wildflowers everywhere, mountain peaks in the background, I felt like skipping. I pictured Heidi tripping up the path, milk pails in hand. But this is Africa and I was at 11,000 feet.

II

Poley poley slowly slowly

This is a walk not a hike

A very long walk

Higher higher — higher still

At 12 thousand feet I pull

Not male energy from my stick

But feminine strength from my heart.

I nurture my body,

Cradle it in my spirit

Gently cajole it into doing

This task for me.

You can do it you can do it

Slowly slowly you can do it.

Up hill and down we stroll

Through alpine meadows and moors

Mountain peaks envelope the plains

Daisies, straw flowers, bluebells

Blink *jambo, Mama* along the path.

Birds chirrup. And all take up the chant.

Yesterday's man in my life, the staff,

Is still beside me but forgotten

Like a divorced husband.

III

You wretched yawning mountain
You filthy rock-spewn plains
Of dun and puce.
You relentless path winding only up
To Kibo Hut
Nausea. Migraine.
Then, rising in bitter cold
And blackest night
To try the summit.
Am I crazed to want
To do this thing?
Decidedly.
As a metaphor for life
It sucks.

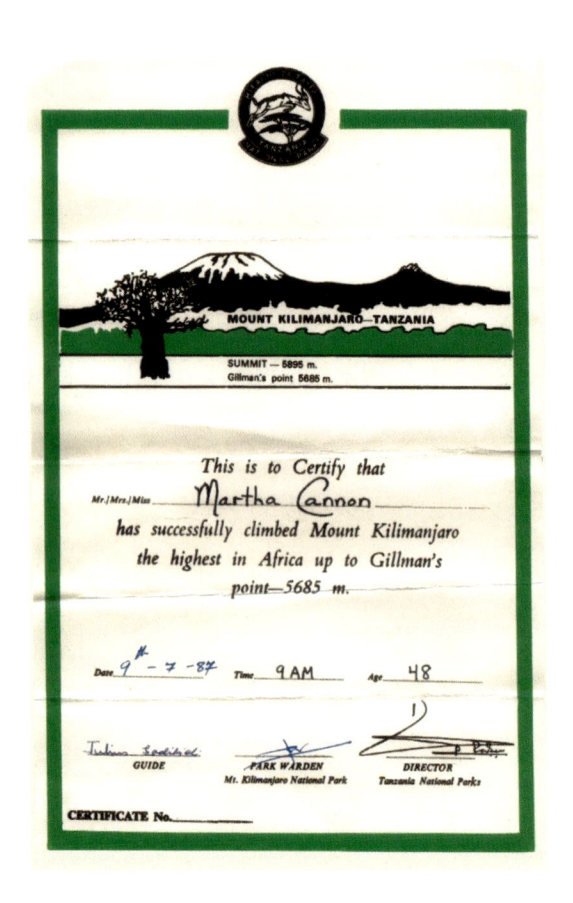

JULY 9

I did it.

THE ODYSSEY OF THE LITTLE RED HEN

This tale is of an odyssey made by a hen
Which occurred long ago,
In the days of Back When.
A Little Red Hen, to be more precise,
Who one day decided it would be nice
To go on a quest
And have an adventure
Away from the nest
Where she'd long been indentured.
So she packed a backpack,
Held terror in check
Turned in her track
To begin a great trek.

Now folks on the farm
Carried on and boo-hooed,
Clucking loudly behind her,
We want to come, too!
But our wings have been clipped
So we're not free like you.
The Little Hen, flipping her feathers,
Said, "Pooh!
We're each of us free
As we choose to be —
No more me than you!"

53

Then how that bird flew,
Seeing such wondrous sights —
Tahiti, Australia,
The Taj in the light
Of the moon,
Kowloon, Malta —
After which soon
She started to falter.
It happened one noon
By an old Buddhist altar
Where the Little Hen mused
On her days as a rover
And learning of truths
That would never go over
Back on the farm.

"The sites I've attended,
Have unbent my mind
But it's time now I mended
What's been left behind —
My garden, my barnyard,
The nest where I brooded —
The best place of all
Is home!" she concluded.

So, home the hen went
Flying West with the sun
One journey spent
The next just begun.

I wrote this in 2001, as a children's book for my grandchildren. I'm remembering now my questing journeys of 1987 and of 1998-99. My conclusion for both — "the best place of all is home."

JOURNAL ENTRY — MAY 10, 2022
(THINKING ABOUT THE PROCESS OF WRITING THIS BOOK)

Here I am, sitting on a pile of smooth rocks, on my journey — in the now of back then 35 years ago, looking tanned and fit, smiling rather proudly — like this chick knows where she is, (I think it's the Seychelle Islands,) is comfortable there, and knows where she's going.

This is a strange exercise, wielding field glasses in reverse, looking back on these significant and life-changing travels of long ago, trying to pull up little representative chunks to share with you. But I find myself drifting off into ponderings, struck by how little I actually remember of the parts of the journey — the pieces. I see this me of then — alone, young, healthy and literally taking on the world. I'm going over the boxes of pictures which I've hardly looked at in the years since. Funny how that is — at the time you click and click, believing you're preserving the experience, recording it so you'll remember it always — and you don't. The small snapshots can't possibly capture anything but the 4 by 6 paper they're on. The takeaway here is, once again, *the whole is greater than the sum of its parts!* My Odyssey of 1987 changed my life, sank into the fiber of my being, and prepared me for a future about which I was clueless at the time. It built the grandest and strongest bridge of my life!!

PEACE CORPS MACEDONIA 1998-1999

It's mid-March 1998, I'm in a hotel room in Chicago watching Laura, my 22-year-old roommate, "suitcase surfing" on her bed — her words — as she looks up at me cheerfully, body splayed prostrate over her huge suitcase, struggling to zip it closed. We've just finished our first day in the Peace Corps, having had input sessions from 9 to 5, and now getting ready to depart for the airport early next morning and fly to Skopje, Macedonia.

I left home, hearth, and family in March 1998 for what was to be a 2+ year stint in the Peace Corps. As a very young mother, back in 1963, my good friend, Nancy, a high school, and college classmate, was one of the first to join the Peace Corps after its founding by John F. Kennedy. Oh, I surely had my nose pasted against that window, caught up in the excellence of the adventure but knee deep at home with four young children. 35 years later, the tiny seed of a dream came to fruition.

The application process was daunting — months of forms to fill out, meetings to attend, questions to answer, and medical examinations to be undertaken. Finally, on a cold winter morning I set off — flew to a hotel in Chicago for two days of staging and then to Frankfurt airport where we connected to a smaller plane which took us to Skopje, the capital of Macedonia. From there we were bussed, exhausted, to the small town of Shtip, an hour from the airport. We were housed overnight in a shabbily inadequate hotel, where my roommate, Alice, one of the older volunteers in the group, a Brit, loudly complained that "There's no bathmat!" (Pronounced bahthmaht.) — to which I replied "Alice, this is the f-ing Peace Corps!!" The woman quit the program less than four months after arrival.

In our cohort there were, of the 28 who started, about ten older members. Over 10 percent of volunteers world-wide are over age 50. I don't know the statistics on how many stay the course for the duration, but in my group only five of us elders lasted to the end, and I might have been one of the quitters had it not been for Liz. About 70 when she enlisted, we became best pals and a mutual support system of 2. We laughed our way through, befriended all the younger PCVs, who called us "the Baba's", Macedonian for grandmothers. We cooked for them, hung out with them, complained with them and roared laughing with them. Many of them fresh out of college, they missed their moms and dads.

One older gentleman left after the first week, unable to reckon with the way the language was being taught. A retired engineer, he had prepared for weeks at home, formulizing the Cyrillic alphabet with his own system for remembering, which did not jibe with the way they were teaching it in our classes. I noticed that the ones who didn't last had each come with an agenda of their own and were invariably disappointed when their private agendas didn't match.

The Peace Corps methodology for teaching language was brilliant. Using flashcards, phonics, songs, repetition, rhyme schemes and fun, most of us soon glommed onto the crazy language which strings consonants together endlessly and turns your tongue into a pneumatic drill trying to pronounce words. (Help! We need a vowel drop!!) Examples: ZDRA-VO (hello);. NO-STRA-VIA (cheers!); My beloved Liz was hopeless with the language and took to saying "Nice driveway!" each time we raised our glasses in a toast — and that was often, as a quite good bottle of local wine sold for less than a dollar a litre.

For the duration of the training program in Shtip, we were housed in individual homes, the families paid by the PC for our board. I was with Blagoy and Dooshka (names spelled phonetically) and their two sons, a daughter-in-law, and small baby. He was a local mail man and she worked in a shirt factory and neither spoke any English. No one in my host home spoke English so I was truly emersed and forced to learn the language quickly.

My art saved me many a lonely hour there. I had my own room, but we all shared the bathroom. One evening the son burst into my room shouting "Visa, Marta, Visa!!" I came to learn that the main reason the family had agreed to take a PCV (Peace Corps Volunteer) was they thought they could obtain a visa to America (very hard to come by in Macedonia) for their son this way. They thought that, as a PC volunteer, I could provide influence. We had a few tense exchanges, but I worked it through with them (with a little help from my PC director) and they soon recognized that I was powerless in the matter. After this, we settled in, I became good friends with Dooshka, despite the language barrier. We laughed, pantomimed, and communicated well enough, having humor and motherhood in common. She couldn't believe I had six children in America — and what the hell was I doing here — so far away from them all?

TREBENYA NA ORIZ
Sorting rice

PENZIONEER
Pensioner

MUSLIMANSKA DEYOYCHAY
Muslim girl

These drawings were among many I made in Macadonia. It saved my sanity during the early days at Blagoy and Dooshka's. I was working on the Pensioner the evening my host's son barged into my room shouting "VISA!" at me. The old gentleman had taken a few of us out on his boat on Lake Ohrid and I snapped a picture of his marvelous face. The activity of drawing created a kind of meditative focus which eased my stress and calmed my mind. It still does

We were abruptly hurried out of Macedonia in late March 1999, when Milosovich was waging war on Kosovo and NATO, with America's sanction, began bombing Bucharest, the Serbian capital. It was feared we would not be safe in our towns, so we were evacuated to Blagoevgrad, Bulgaria, where we were housed in a large hotel (it had bathmats) near the American University campus. After one month of not knowing, we were flown home, compelled to leave our sites, the work we had begun, the new friends we had met.

After my return to America, I wrote the following in my journal. I had just framed the above three drawings and was reflecting on one of them.

JOURNAL ENTRY — DECEMBER 1, 1999
(BACK IN AMERICA SIX MONTHS AFTER EVACUATION)

I connected to this woman sorting rice. So intent was she at her task that nothing on earth seemed more important. Her gentle, Zen-like concentration was a model for me and as I worked on the drawing, I worked on being more fully present in Macedonia. I tried to push aside the homesickness and loneliness and focus on my purpose there, even while not knowing precisely what that purpose was. I still don't! Many days it was just to take care of myself, do my laundry, walk to the market for groceries, come back and prepare a meal — small, inconsequential tasks — Zen and the art of self-maintenance.

As I look back now on my year in Macedonia, I'm filled with mixed and conflicted emotions. I met one family who became like my own family to me but made few other friends outside of my PC cohort. My students were mostly a joy and I know I made at least a small positive impact on them. At Christmas I directed a pageant with 60 students singing carols and reading the Christmas story in three languages: English, French and Macedonian. (Angels We Have Heard On High became si-sloosh — ee -may ang-gel-ee-tay) It was a magical event, and the kids (high school students) were practically levitating with pride afterwards — and then we all went out for pizza. I accomplished other small things, but there was the rapid retreat in March, right after the NATO action against Serbia began and it was feared that we would become overnight pariahs in our communities — the hatred between ethnic Macedonians (Eastern Orthodox Christians) and Albanian Muslims was centuries old and now re-ignited into fierce nationalism. We left projects begun but unfinished and had no time for closure with our Macedonian friends, students, and colleagues.

I look back on my PC experience and wonder — what was that all about?? But there is rice to be sorted today and life back here in America, as in Macedonia, demands my full attention. I expect the wonderings will take care of themselves in good time.

And they have. From my present perch in Elderhood, I exult at having had this adventure, of having gotten to immerse myself in an utterly alien culture and flourished in it, at having made good friends with bright-eyed, idealistic youngsters, my fellow PC volunteers, fresh out of college, and been on a level playing field with them. I would take the tortuous three-hour bus trip from my town of Prilep to Skopje, winding through the mountains, to my friend Liz's apartment, where we'd spend the weekend with a gang of young volunteers. I would cook, Liz didn't — she referred to me as the "cooking Baba." We'd drink beer and wine and swap stories, kvetch a lot and be mercilessly irreverent as we shared about our respective experiences. The living room floor would be covered with wall to wall sleeping bags — fortunately, there were twin beds in the bedroom for Liz and me.

Mark came to visit from Germany in July. He bought me a bike. My apartment is the pink one. We painted the sun on my balcony wall — it looks a little homesick.

My Peace Corps assignment was to teach English and Economics in an Economics Highschool in Prilep, Macedonia, where I moved in June 1998, after graduating from the training program in Shtip. I spent a long, hot summer left to my own devices and began teaching in late August.

Hanging out in Liz's apartment with PCVs: Liz, Tracy, Rob and Jody.

Some students visiting my apartment, "stan," in Macedonian.

My beloved Petreski family — Drashko and Sonchitsa and their children, Emmy and Christian. They lived downstairs in my apartment building, adopted me as a surrogate Grammy and saved my life. I was the only American in the city of Prilep and was terribly homesick. They invited me for dinner often, we drank many a "nostravya" toast, Sonchitsa became my language tutor and the children came up nearly every day to play on my computer. I have returned twice to Macedonia since 1999 and stayed with them. The Petreskis are my friends for life. Christian is now married and Emmy, soon to be married, lives in New Jersey. Her parents are coming to the U.S. for the wedding and we will have a reunion here. I love my life!!

It was a twenty-minute walk to get to my school. The houses in late summer are bedecked with peppers (pee-pair-key) drying, as well as tobacco. A national pastime from late august to mid-october is the making of AJVAR — pronounced Aye-var, a red pepper spread that is delicious beyond description. Everyone grows peppers for ajvar, virtually every household in the country produces their supply for the year, the making of which creates an aroma which lingers over all of Macedonia through November.

I celebrated my 60th birthday in Macedonia with two young volunteers in my group. Nicole, on the left, was turning 21 and Robert, in the middle, 29. Everything was so inexpensive there, that we could easily afford to hire a boat for our 110TH BIRTHDAY BASH. Everybody brought pot-luck food. We sailed around Lake Ohrid, on the MAKEDONJA, drank buckets of beer, wine and rakia (the local firewater.) An epic birthday! An unforgettable milestone.

Nicole and Laura (the suitcase surfer)

Nicole cutting the birthday cake

I've been questing or resting — one way or another for most of my adult life — from the twenty-nine-year-old mother of six, sitting in the Quaker Meeting House to the middle-aged virgin mother of six, hanging from a rappelling rope. Writing poems has always been a part of my quest — to gain space from an issue, ask the right questions, or find resolution.

I have also sought professional council — another avenue of quest. Thayer Greene, a wise and wonderful Jungian psychologist in New York city, was my therapist for several years during the rough passage of my marriage's end. For Christmas that first year, I gave him this poem, attached to a dowel like a pinwheel. You'll have to spin the book around to follow it.

my therapist likes me whatta relief I was beginning to wonder when poking and probing my issues with something less delicate than a surgeon's knife he'd offer me no more solace than a box of tissues and an empathic look at least I took it as empathic 3 talking through that door raw wound walking out but I know I'm less neurotic now 'cuz I'm not going to miss my therapist's circle any more than I miss meeting with so much sorrow and wit glad

> Oh what a gift would He give us, to see ourselves as others see us.
> ROBERT BURNS

Some questing discoveries are anything but pleasant. Besides weekly private sessions, Thayer facilitated a weekly one-hour group session, consisting of a diverse group of his clients. Pam, one of the participants, called us "intimate strangers," an apt name, for we knew each other's deep private pain, shame, and secrets, but had no contact or social interaction outside of group. The effectiveness of the group process was receiving honest feedback from others, all of us going through our individual processes of uncovering our authentic selves — selves we often mask with people pleasing public personae. I was a master mask wearer and didn't even know it!

Here's a journal entry from December 30, 1986 — I was 47:

> Tonight, in group Jeanne confronted me, very gently and carefully, that she finds me inauthentic — not giving the whole picture — only showing my shiny side — and she has experienced me this way from the beginning. Somehow, I knew this was coming and a piece of me knows it to be true. Pam, more confrontive, then chimed in that I come in and "throw my tinsel around the room — but what's behind it?"

Good question — which I addressed in an entry a few days later:

> I realize that there is a very deep, wounded part of me which I go to great lengths to defend against. I am just now realizing that — and that part is what keeps a large chunk of me quite inaccessible to myself and to others. The shiny, razzle dazzle side is easy to keep up front. But all the efforts of my ego will not effect change. Change will effect itself as we get at the wounded little me — the introverted, private part that I'm ashamed of. I want to be integrated. I want to become 3-dimensional. The shit of it all seems to me that so much is so unconscious. It's not fair — so much behavior based on wounds buried over and pushed into the unconscious — causing behavior which kills relationships, spirit and certainly maims one's capacity to give and to love. GOD!!! WHERE ARE YOU IN ALL THIS?? Are You here — or is this kind of a cosmic joke where the laugh is on us blind mice and see how we run. SHIT!!

I wrote many poems during these days — trying to find myself, trying to find God, trying to work it out. Here are some.

MEDITATION ON "LITTLE ME"

Look at Little Me
Notice where she's at
Breathe her in and
Breathe her out
Sure, she can be a brat
But mostly if abandoned
Or feeling reprimanded.

Give her some attention —
Don't ignore the call
Pick her up and hug her
She's just a kid, after all.

RISKY BUSINESS

T'is a challenging task
This removal of masks —
I've been at it for seventy years.
Back then we used smiles
To conceal woes and wiles
And put up a shield
Against fears.

But the day comes, my dears —
Around middle age —
The seal breaks, the mask slips
And you're up to your hips
In detritus and rage —

A time to get wise
Drop the disguise
And set yourself free.
It happened to me.

TOUGH TALK FROM AN INNER CHILD

If I'm a little loser
Let's get it straight who's who here
I hate it stuck behind your screen
With you out like a beauty queen
Acting serene and always clean —
That's mean!

Well, I'm a mess and guess
I'll stay that way.
But who's to say I'm not OK!
I may be messy but I'm real
Why won't you look at me and feel
What's in my heart —
Fix my broken parts,
Mix us
We could start again
Like new

If I'm a loser —
You are, too!

REMEMBERING

She was just four or five
when I gave her the boot
That curly-haired child
In a new blue sun suit
It was checkered,
With lace ruffles looping
Across her bottom.
God, she was cute
Pirouetting so proudly
Giggling then shouting
A little too loudly,
"Look at me! Look at Me!
Aren't I the best?"
But receiving replies,
Well, you know the rest
—
The decries and the glares
And the small soul undressed.
I was there, in fact helped
To suppress her
And banish her
Where I hoped no one
Would guess her—

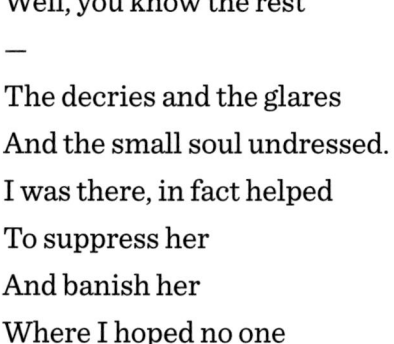

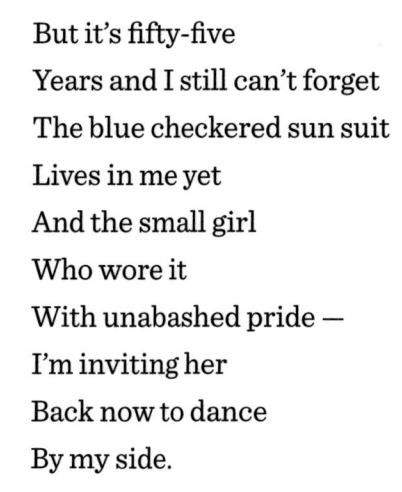

But it's fifty-five
Years and I still can't forget
The blue checkered sun suit
Lives in me yet
And the small girl
Who wore it
With unabashed pride —
I'm inviting her
Back now to dance
By my side.

REMEMBERING

She was just four or five
when I gave her the boot
That curly-haired child
In a new blue sun suit
It was checkered,
With lace ruffles looping
Across her bottom.
God, she was cute
Pirouetting so proudly
Giggling then shouting
A little too loudly,
"Look at me! Look at Me!
Aren't I the best?"
But receiving replies,
Well, you know the rest
—
The decries and the glares
And the small soul undressed.
I was there, in fact helped
To suppress her
And banish her
Where I hoped no one
Would guess her—

But it's fifty-five
Years and I still can't forget
The blue checkered sun suit
Lives in me yet
And the small girl
Who wore it
With unabashed pride —
I'm inviting her
Back now to dance
By my side.

Interlude

OOMHHS

JOURNAL ENTRY — MARCH 20, 2022

I've been drawing these "Out Of My Head Heads" for years — my way of doodling. This morning I read a quote from the naturalist, John Burroughs:

To have a mind eager to know the great truths and broad enough to take them in, and not get lost in the maze of apparent contradictions is undoubtedly the highest good.

This OOMHH looks like she may have that kind of mind — open, curious, serious. I mounted the image on a piece of scrap paper and then noticed the anchor — the lady is grounded.

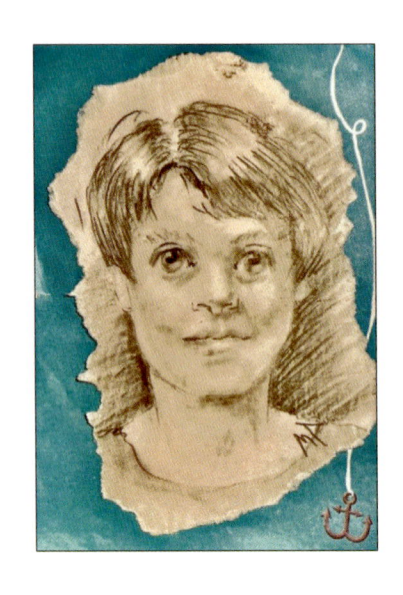

I used this one as a lesson in one of my portraiture classes — had the students create a portrait of someone who does not exist. It's a great exercise, a quiz in how much you've learned in class. Fun to become God of the page and create a being. Fun because you never know who's going to show up!

Interlude

OOMHHS

JOURNAL ENTRY — MARCH 20, 2022

I've been drawing these "Out Of My Head Heads" for years — my way of doodling. This morning I read a quote from the naturalist, John Burroughs:

To have a mind eager to know the great truths and broad enough to take them in, and not get lost in the maze of apparent contradictions is undoubtedly the highest good.

This OOMHH looks like she may have that kind of mind — open, curious, serious. I mounted the image on a piece of scrap paper and then noticed the anchor — the lady is grounded.

I used this one as a lesson in one of my portraiture classes — had the students create a portrait of someone who does not exist. It's a great exercise, a quiz in how much you've learned in class. Fun to become God of the page and create a being. Fun because you never know who's going to show up!

NEW YEAR VILLANELLE

FOR MARK

The night was black without a star
to punctuate the winter sky.
I did not wonder how you are

But slept instead far far
away — my restfulness belied
the blackness of your night without a star.

You took your life too far
from here and closed in on your own storm's eye.
And now I wonder where you are

and are you peaceful, son, or are
you hanging somewhere in the deep,
no more a blinding star

but now a meteor
burnt out with no goodbye,
no dropping ball, no auld lang syne,
no revelry for you — but only sleep
while far away
I did not wonder how you are
that winter night without a star

Another self-portrait — a difficult one. This was a drawing I made in my journal six months after the death of my son, Mark, a time of grieving beyond grieving. He was fifty, suffered from debilitating depression, lived in Europe, and took his life on New Year's Eve 2013. A brilliant, charismatic man, an unbelievably talented artist — a terrible loss, but somehow, we understood how he was simply unable to carry on.

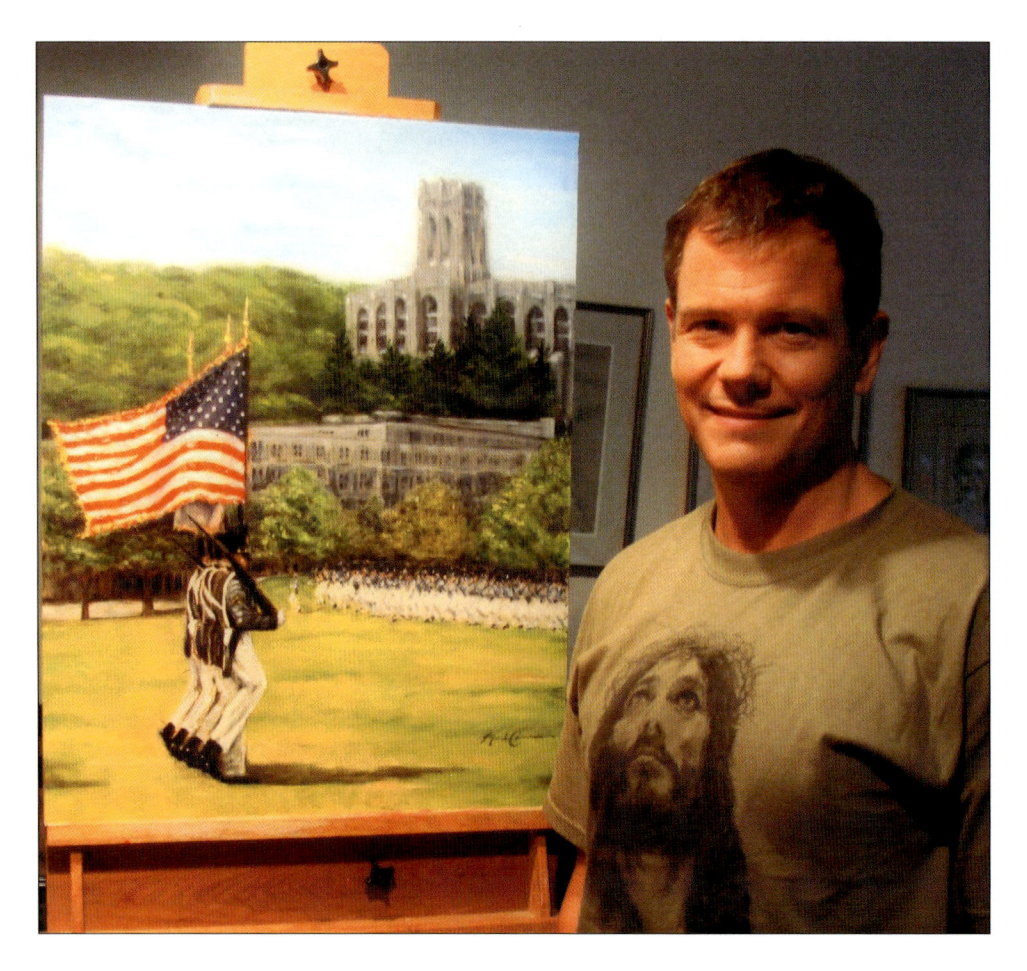

My candle burns at both ends;

It will not last the night;

But ah, my foes, and oh, my friends—

It gives a lovely light!

EDNA ST. VINCENT MILLAY

I drew this one on a cold winter day in 2016. I was home at my drawing board, determined to create a no holds barred, realistic self-portrait. A poem followed quickly on the heels of my efforts.

RELENTLESS

Courageously she renders
Each cranny and nook
Not for a minute
Lets self off the hook
Or ponders relentless
Time in the glass
Remembering the lass
She was long ago.
No! Not before
She explores
Every wattle and wrink,
Does she pack up her pencils
And have a stiff drink.

SELF-PORTRAITS

Just as I have drawn innumerable Out of My Head Heads through the years, I've probably produced even more self-portraits. This is an invaluable exercise, giving the artist time, on her own terms, to study study study human facial anatomy and expression — an opportunity to bring to life that face in the mirror which happens to be her own, and to learn to still or ignore the critical ego voices, telling her how old, fat, wrinkled etc she is. Walt Whitman said, "I contain multitudes." The best part of the self-portrait exercise is seeing who shows up.

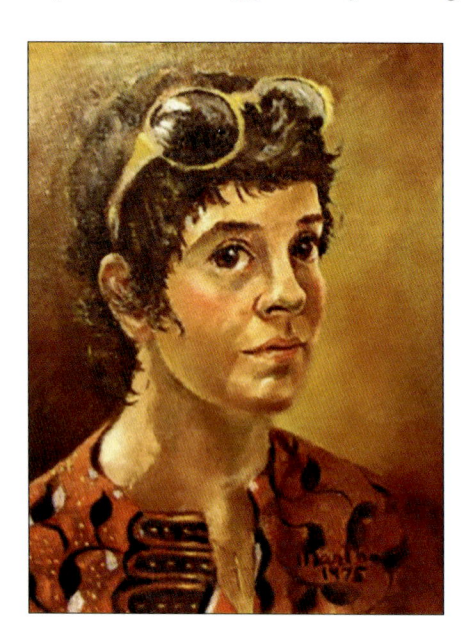

This one showed up in 1975, back when I was a thirty-something year old mother of six, commuting to New York twice a week to take classes at the Art Students League — a life-changing endeavor. I was painting in oils at the time — have since switched to acrylics — dries faster and easier to clean up.

Here are a few more Marthas who've shown up more recently...

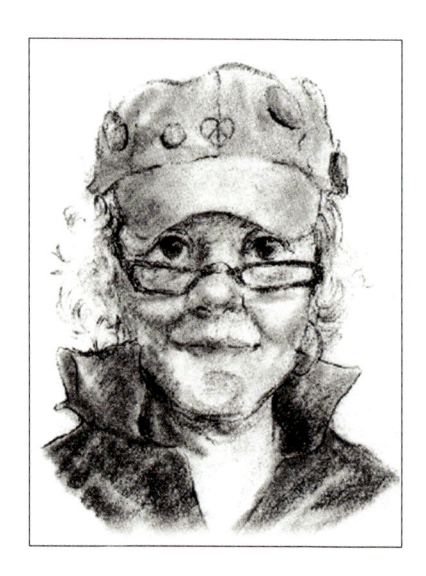

77

THE WAY UP

I have had to climb down
a thousand ladders
until I could reach
out my hand
to the little
clod of earth
I am.

CARL JUNG

I aspire to becoming one who has learned to gestate and give birth to her own subjectivity.
ADRIENNE RICH

Our basic core of goodness is our true Self
Its center of gravity is God
The acceptance of our basic goodness
Is a quantum leap in the spiritual journey.
THOMAS KEATING

WHO AM I NOT

All great spirituality is a journey
which teaches about letting go of what
you don't need and who you are not.
RICHARD ROHR

Who am I not?
The needy one
Who dreads rejection;
The beady-eyed one
Who demands perfection;
The diva who revels
In every attention,
Lighting her face, a blush,
At mere mention of her name —
All the same, and many more.
God, I implore you,
If these I am not
How far have I got?
And how do I hush
all these "Nots"
Who show up?
Who am I, God?
And who am I not?

SOUL GARDENING

Dig deep
through dense clods
of moist self.
Get messy.
Let earthworms
till the way
to angels
who live down here —
and not up top
where smiling faces
bloom along the wall.

OBSERVATIONS OF AN ART TEACHER AT THE SENIOR CENTER

One hurtful remark
From a person of yore —
A teacher, a parent,
A sibling, or more —
Can so wound a child
That the sore
Doesn't heal
And fifty years later
I see and feel
A small soul in pain
From hurt carelessly dealt,
And still freshly felt:
> Don't draw, you've no talent
> Don't sing, you're off-key
> Don't dance — you're too clumsy

... And the artist in you
And the dancer in me
Have ourselves labeled
As ones who can not —
The inner despot
Has its way!
It's time, friends, today.
We all have a choice
To hush that harsh voice
And try once again.
If not now — when.

JOURNAL DOODLING

I contain multitudes.
WALT WHITMAN

Time heals in time. My brother-in-law, a physician, coined a phrase which expresses it well: "tincture of time." Making art helped. I painted this picture shortly after Mark died. I just wanted to paint water; there was no image I was copying, only the image in my head. The little boat emerged, making its way across rough waters. I called the painting *Red Sails on a Stormy Sea* and the sea was surely sad and stormy. But the little boat was making it through. I created a number of "stormy sea" paintings while grieving and, like the little boat, I was making my way through. This one hangs on my wall as a daily reminder — more of making it through than of storminess.

The final image is a "portrait prayer" I made on the third anniversary of Mark's death. The grief lingers but the seas had calmed a bit, as had I.

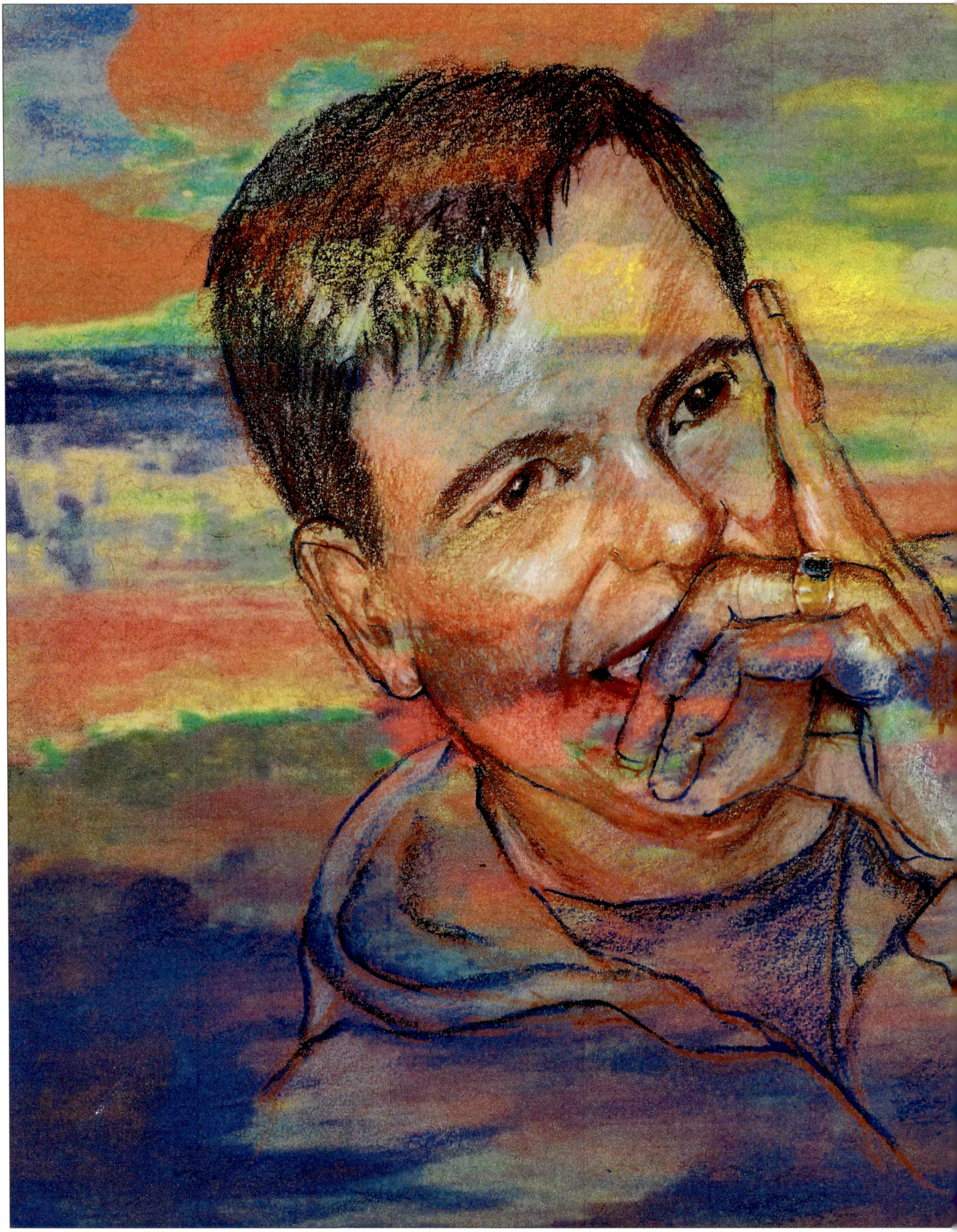

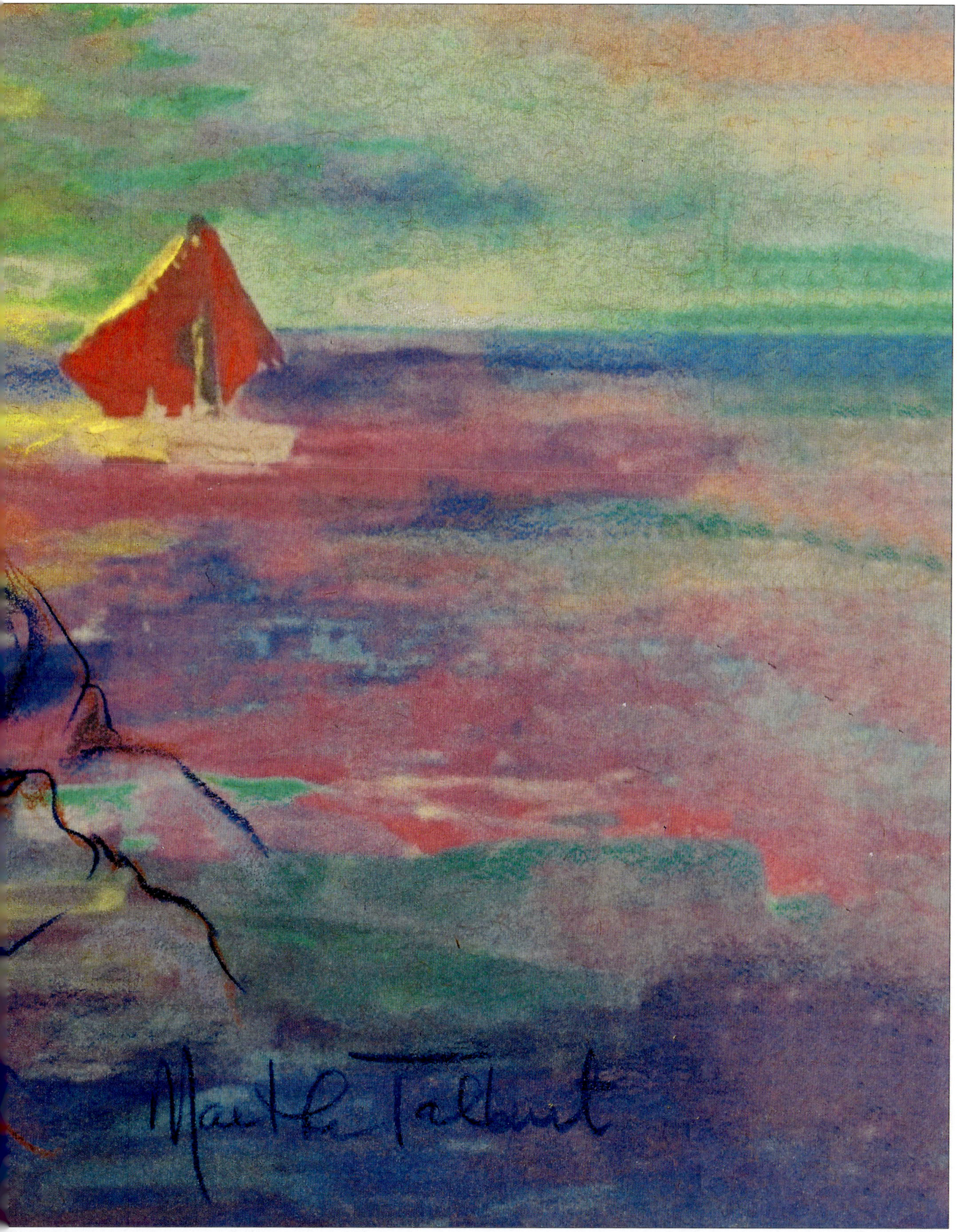

In my late seventies, I got a little rescue dog and named her Zoey. Never having had a dog, I was understandably nervous about being up to the task. But I had watched several of my grown children being enriched by having dogs in their families and I decided it was time to check it out. Enter Zoey. Here are some Zoems.

ODE TO ZOEY — MY RESCUE DOG

My Zoey gambols on our strolls every day.
A merry old soul, the vets say
She's twelve years — or more
But you'd never tell
As she bolts out the door
To take in every smell
Nose to ground, like sweeping a floor
Nothing left unexplored.
As one who had never before
Owned a dog, I'm told
I have rescued her generously.
Together five years and friends, now I see
That it is Zoey who is rescuing me.

ZOEY KNOWS

Zoey knows
With her nose
I can only suppose
The mysteries she probes
As we go on our rounds,
Nose sweeping the ground,
I cannot know all she takes in
For what Zoey has found
When she's bounding around
Can only confound homo sapiens

ABSTRACT RANDOM

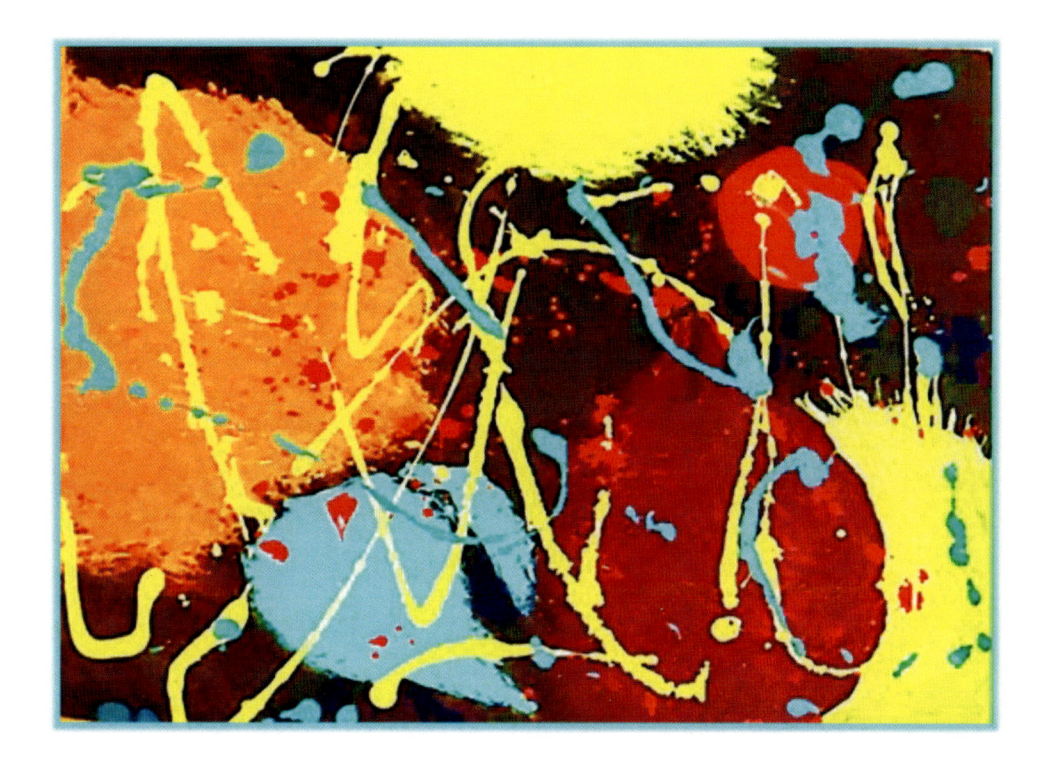

This is a painting I made many years ago, which sits now on top of the corner bookshelf in my studio — overlooking the action down here. I had pre-painted a canvas warm black, dropped it onto the floor and began shplopping and dribbling colors I liked onto the surface. The shapes took on an interesting weirdness against the dark background, but I recall loving what I was doing — having fun in a devil-may-care manner — just letting loose. The grand finale was squirting the yellow and teal from nozzled bottles and creating what I now see as a marvelous dance.

I had never really created an abstract before and was pleased with the energy of it. I laughingly called it FAMLIAGE — because it made me think about the unpredictability and seeming randomness of the many interrelationships in my own life, as well as in my large, now grown-up family.

Recently I discovered the work of Professor Anthony Gregorc, from the University of Connecticut, whose study has been how people think and methods they employ working their way through life. Certainly, we don't all think alike, problem solve alike, or work through stuff alike. Gregorc suggests four thinking and learning styles and created a test to help folks determine their particular operating systems, which are: Concrete sequential. Concrete random. Abstract random. Abstract sequential.

I took the test and guess what I found out — as if I didn't know already on some instinctive level. I am ABSTRACT RANDOM AND CONCRETE RANDOM!! Hardly a SEQUENTIAL in sight! The painting says it all! Briefly, here is how it looks:

CONCRETE SEQUENTIAL

This learner likes:
- Order
- Logical sequence
- Following directions, predictability
- Getting facts

They learn best when:
- They have a structured environment
- They can rely on others to complete the task
- Are faced with predictable situations
- Can apply ideas in pragmatic ways

What's hard for them?
- Working in groups
- Discussions that seem to have no specific point
- Working in an unorganized environment
- Following incomplete or unclear directions
- Working with unpredictable people
- Dealing with abstract ideas
- Demands to "use your imagination"
- Questions with no right or wrong answers.

ABSTRACT SEQUENTIAL

This learner likes:
- His/her point to be heard
- Analyzing situations before acting or making a decision
- Applying logic in solving or fining solutions to problems

They learn best when:
- They have access to experts or references
- Placed in stimulating environments
- Able to work alone

What's hard for them?
- Being forced to work with those of differing views
- Too little time to deal with a subject thoroughly
- Repeating the same tasks over and over
- Lots of specific rules and regulations
- "Sentimental" thinking
- Expressing emotions
- Being diplomatic when convincing others
- Not monopolizing a conversation

CONCRETE RANDOM

This learner likes:
- Experimenting to find answers
- Taking risks
- Using their intuition
- Solving problems independently

They learn best when:
- They're able to use trial & error approaches
- They're able to compete with others
- They're given the opportunity to work through problems by themselves

What's hard for them?
- Restrictions and limitations
- Formal reports
- Routines
- Re-doing anything once it's done
- Keeping detailed records
- Showing how they got an answer
- Choosing only one answer
- Having no options

ABSTRACT RANDOM

This learner likes:
- Listening to others
- Bringing harmony to group situations
- Establishing healthy relationships with others
- Focusing on the issues at hand

They learn best when:
- in a personalized environment
- given broad or general guidelines
- able to maintain friendly relationships
- able to participate in group activities

What's hard for them?
- Having to explain or justify feelings
- Competition
- Working with dictatorial/authoritarian personalities
- Working in a restrictive environment
- Working with people who don't seem friendly
- Concentrating on one thing at a time
- Giving exact details
- Accepting even positive criticism

I'm spending time on this because it's been such an important discovery! For most of my adult life I've been trying to find "the big system in the sky" — which has always eluded me. Of course!

Systematic, linear thinking is not my style — I'm hardwired to be random! And as I've been working away on this book — in my own inimitable fashion — I've been haunted by old toxic introjects to be more systematic, organized, tidy, etc. — demon voices! This new input has freed me up to follow the process of getting this work together in my own way — there is no one right way! Which gets me back to Antonio Machado's wise poem:

PATHMAKER

> Your footsteps are the path
> And nothing more;
> Pathmaker, there is no path.
> You make the path by walking.
> By walking, you make the path.
>
> ANTONIO MACHADO

I have kept the painting (even though tempted to paint over it) and as I look at it now, I see how good a visual metaphor it is and how well it describes my life. The dark background is the negative field in which I operated for so many years in a not good marriage (certainly unbeknownst or named as such at the time.) The colorful forms represent children, raising family, friendships, commitments, interests, challenges, loves, seasons, etc. — and over it all dances my spirituality — a paramount reality in my life since forever. And a dance it is — the sparkling bright yellow pervades the canvas — it is the thread of William Stafford's THE WAY IT IS poem. I have long resonated deeply to this poem and now I relate to it even more right here in my studio in a painting that emerged from my deep subconscious and told my story long before I could know it.

THE WAY IT IS

There's a thread you follow. It goes among
things that change. But it doesn't change.
People wonder about what you are
pursuing.
You have to explain about the thread.
But it is hard for others to see.
While you hold it you can't get lost.
Tragedies happen; people get hurt
or die; and you suffer and get old.
Nothing you do can stop time's unfolding.
You don't ever let go of the thread.

WILLIAM STAFFORD

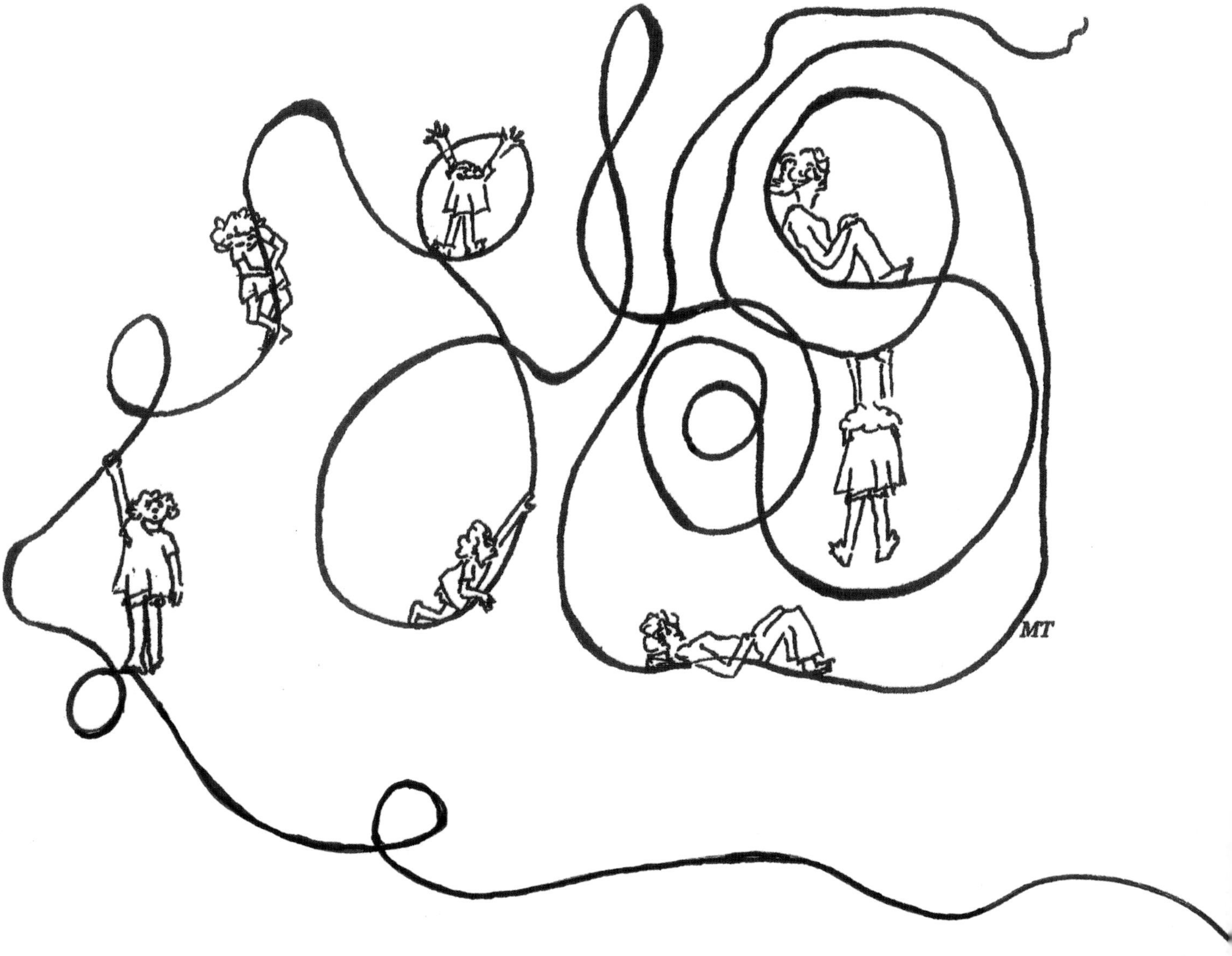
MT

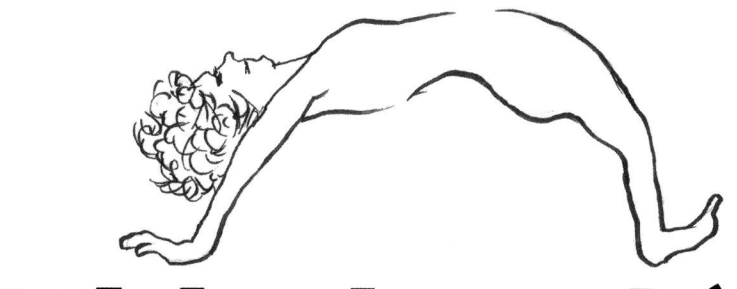

Elderhood(y)

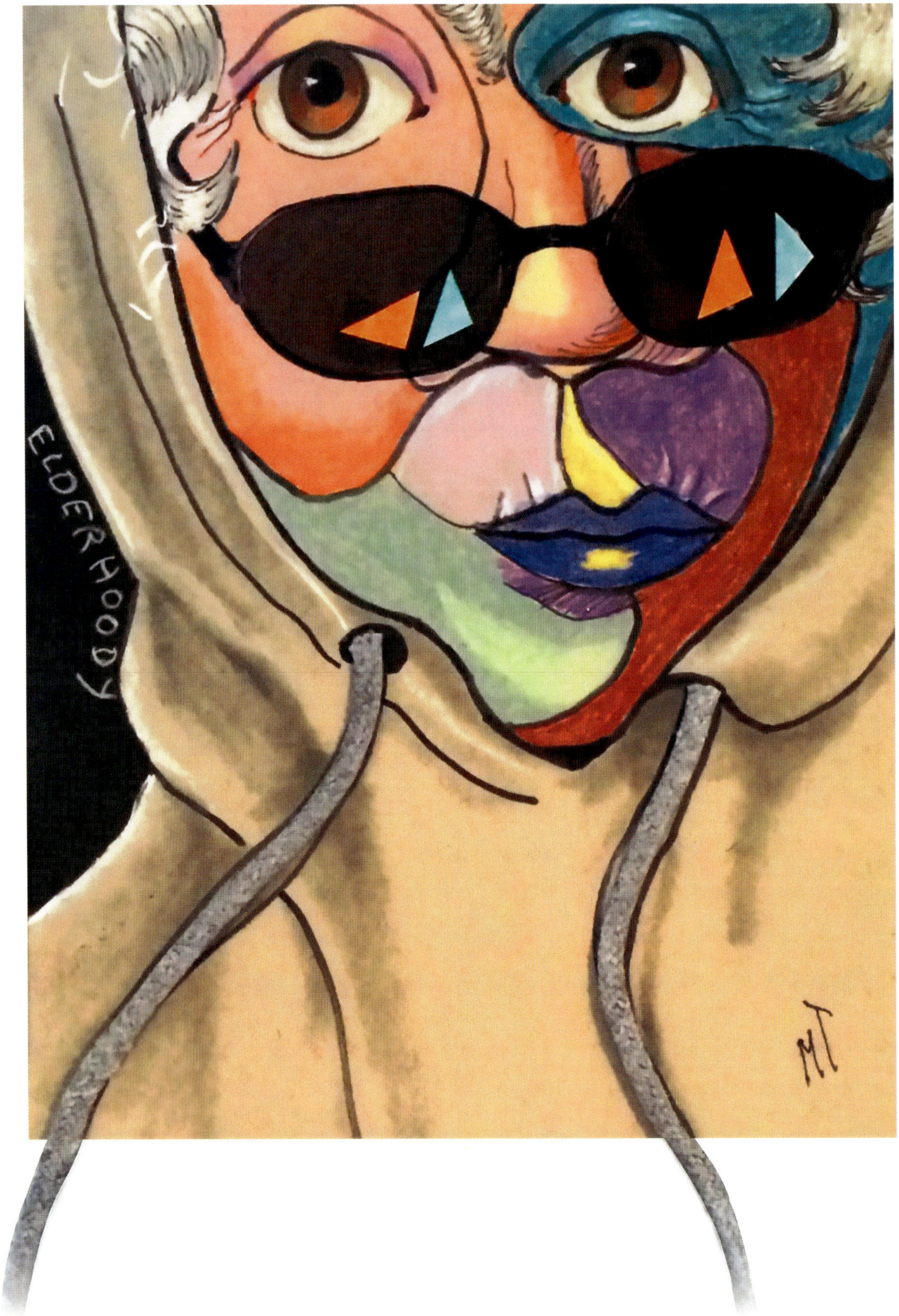
ELDERHOODY
MT

I sketched this in my journal on August 23, 2018 — one month before my 80th birthday. She looks a little wistful, pondering what's ahead while clueless about what's ahead. What was behind her, though, was plenty.

I ended my second marriage in late 2017, moved in with my beloved daughter, Sarah, who offered me refuge, and was divorced in mid-April 2018. I had remarried two years after returning from the Peace Corps. The marriage was a kind of mutual rescue operation. It was not bad, but ultimately it was not good enough. We did some marvelous traveling together but eventually grew apart and, at 79, I decided I could not spend the rest of my life in "not good enough." I wrote the following poem in the divorce court. Our case came up last, so I had several hours to attend and observe about eighteen unpairings before ours.

AT THE DIVORCE COURT WHERE WE COME TO SAY I DON'T BUT END UP WITH I DO

We sit in court like in a church
In rigid rows of oaken pews
And walls that match, the room suffused
With air of golden hue.
Oyez. Oyez, cries the clerk;
The judge comes in, we stand.
A white-haired priestess robed in black —
Pink coffee cup in hand —
Surveys her congregation
Of former lovers, couples who
Process up to her station
Not to say I do.

This is church, but in reverse,
Serving folks whose lives got worse
Since the time they swore
Those words to different priests
And now, their ardor long deceased,
They're praying *Nevermore!*

When finally, our case comes up
The white-haired judge inquires
Do we null our nuptials freely?
Are all affidavits true?
And do you to it swear? she queries.
We reply — I do.

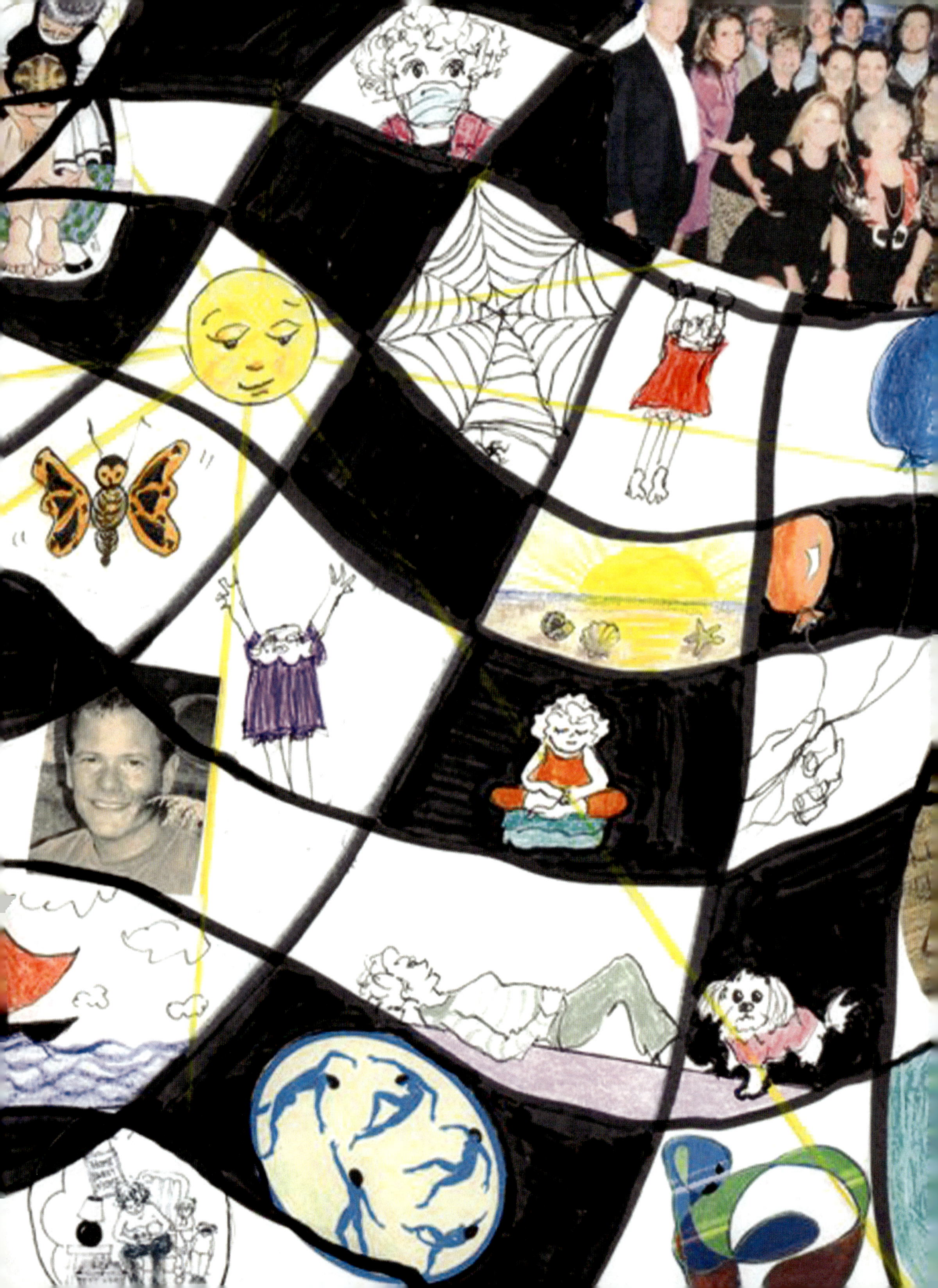

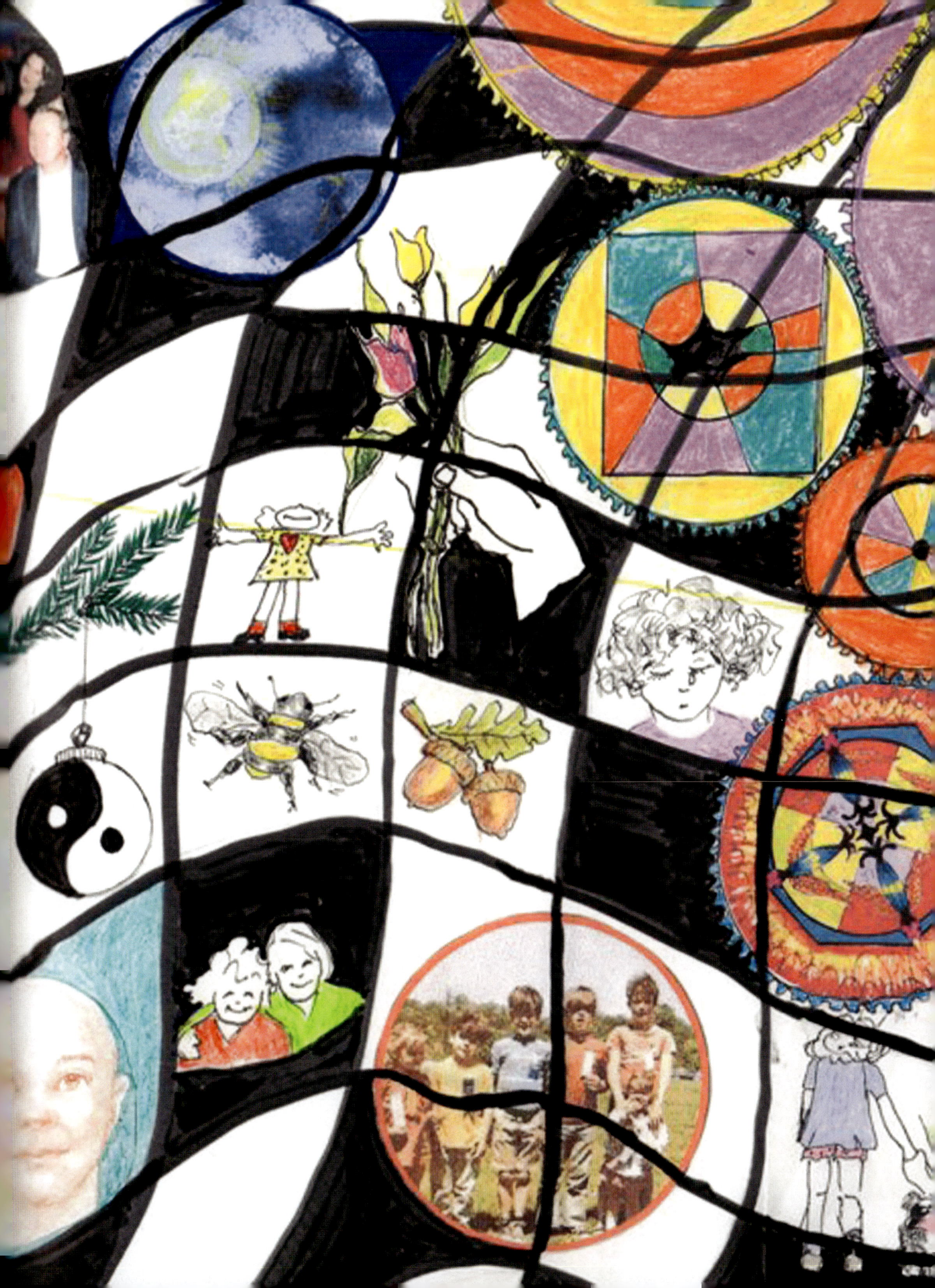

"Grammy — keep? Give away? Throw away?" Madeleine, my nineteen-year-old granddaughter, queries me as I stand, utterly confused, amid mountains of stuff in the move from a Stratford, Connecticut condo to an apartment in Ridgefield. I don't dare dither, as this grandchild brooks no interference, and we roll through the piles smoothly and efficiently. Thank God for grandchildren!

So, on the eve of my 80th birthday, I had achieved the impossible, divorced a husband, sold a condo, moved into a new apartment and begun to prepare for another semester, teaching art classes about 16 to 20 hours a week. I had been teaching classes in and around Ridgefield for 12 years — a source of joy, satisfaction, and delight for me — as well as a lot of work!

Then, there was also the delight of looking forward to my big birthday bash, which was to take place on September 9th, a little ahead of the actual date, to accommodate Sarah, who was catering the event. Family and dear friends from all over the country arrived the day before and, on that day, early in the morning while walking my dog, I had an ischemic stroke in the cerebellum of my brain. The sidewalk tipped, dumped me, and I landed, to spend my birthday party day in the Danbury Connecticut hospital.

What saved me was something called TPA — the "clot buster' drug (tissue plasminogen activator) which, if administered within 4 hours of an ischemic (clot based) stroke, dissolves the clot and minimizes its effects. Lucky me — and, irony of ironies, my nephew, Dr. Christopher Cannon, is one of the scientists who developed the drug which probably saved my life and most certainly spared me from some awful results. I landed precisely where I belonged, as did my party invitees, many of whom gathered at Sarah's house and had — I call it — *a family reunion over my live body* which was being well taken care of in the ICU unit.

I have come to think of all this as a "stroke of good fortune," that relieved me of a way too busy schedule, gave me pause to retire from same, to rest, to think, and to be everlastingly grateful. Many journal entries and poems — of course — ensued during my recovery.

JOURNAL ENTRY — SEPTEMBER 15, 2018
(ONE WEEK AFTER STROKE)

99

THE BATTLE OF MY BRAIN

The sidewalk tilted, I spilt on a hill
When my brain drained.
I remember it all. It happened last fall.
Strained Brain,

Unable to face one more day of my pace,
Ordained
An ischemic to erase
Lame Brain.

Schemes got cancelled that day,
As did the runaway train.
Calendars emptied. Plans went away.
Constrained Brain

Was left in the wake of the clot.
But I was not trained
To be still, as was the will of
Brave Brain

Who knew it was best
To restrain me —
To rest and
Sustain Brain!

This is a form of poetry called a ghazal (pronounced guzzle) that I learned about when taking a class at the library several months after my stroke. It was taught by my beloved niece, Pam, who is an outstanding poet and teacher, and who has been invaluable in the editing process of this book.

Writing poems, journaling and sketching has been central to my recovery process. The ability to write and draw has not been affected by the stroke. Oddly enough, however, some small motor controls have — like putting my earrings in, using chopsticks, or cracking an egg. Funny.

The recovery process went on for over a year, during which time my energies were greatly depleted. I rested a lot — but often with journal or sketch book in hand. Here is more of the work (play) which emerged, starting with a few mandalas. I love making mandalas!

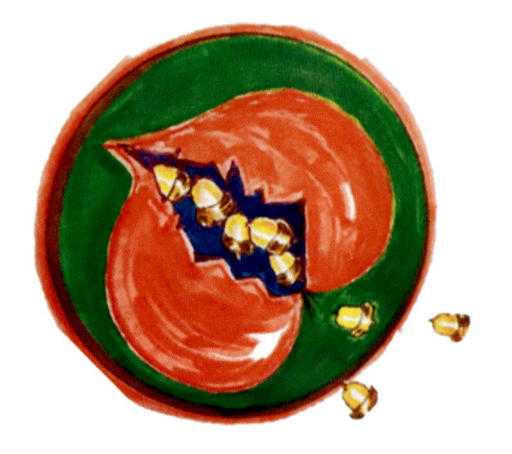

This acorn mandala is among the many I created during my recovery. Acorns and oak trees have long been powerful metaphors for me. I wear an acorn tattoo proudly on my shoulder. My granddaughter, Gabrielle, a musician, asked me a few weeks before her 16th birthday to soften her Mommy to the fact that all she wanted for her birthday was a sixteenth note tattooed on her shoulder. As I already had a tattoo (wings on my heel — got it on my 63rd birthday), she figured I'd be a good softener. I was. We celebrated a tri-generational tattooing event — Gabrielle got her musical note, I got my acorn, and Sarah, a sun mandala. It was a memorable birthday. I wrote the following celebratory poem shortly afterwards.

TALE OF THE ACORN AND THE CHIP

TO MY GRANDCHILDREN

Gather round me, children,
Listen closely, take a tip
From the story I must tell you
Of the acorn and the chip.

The former fell beneath an oak,
One of many dropped that day.
A little girl was passing by,
Who heard the acorn say —

Look around you, girl, and see
These wonders on the ground —
A thousand tiny ones like me,
All chances to rebound

And grow and re-create
Our Mother Oak provides.
Can you not appreciate
Her kindness? You decide!

Nothing doing! a wood chip intruded,
Stuck there in the dirt,
The things this silly seed's concluded —
Hogwash! I assert

That acorns are mere droppings
From this mighty tree —
Off which, I might add, I'm a chip —
Look down here — at ME!

By then the little girl had passed
The acorn and the chip,
Grown up, got old, before she grasped
That day's apprenticeship

And moral of this tale —
Which has run on a bit:
An acorn on your shoulder
Is much better than a chip.

(WRITTEN IN HONOR OF THE GREAT TRI-GENERATIONAL TATTOOING EVENT)

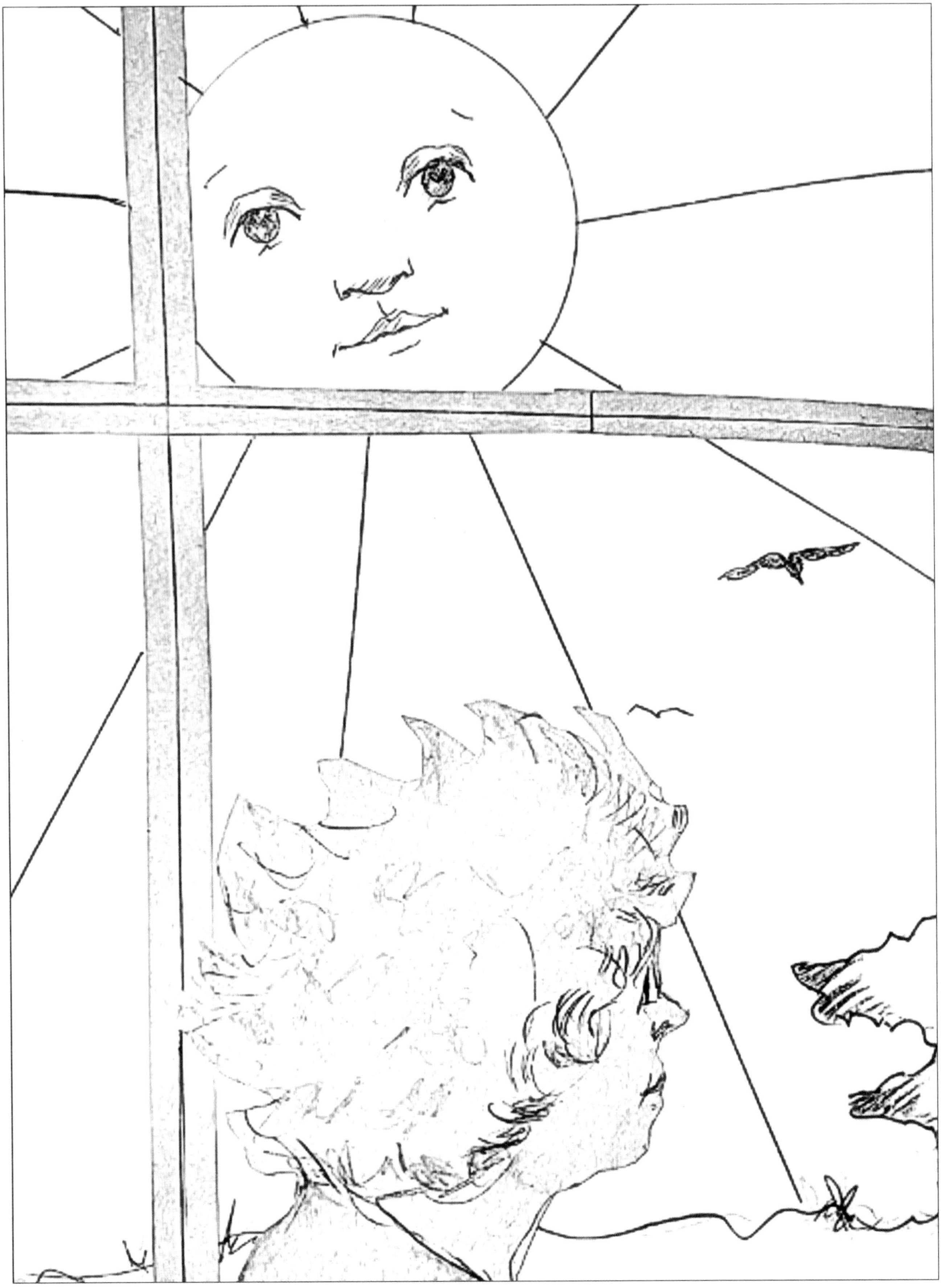

IN GOOD TIME

I lead a good life
In my living room chair,
Lately home base
From where I face
A parallel world
In one small space.
Through my window now I see
Cardinals, juncos, chickadees,
Busy chipmunks, sparrows (of course),
Woodpeckers, nuthatches,
A blue jay who forces
His way on the feeder.
The others, with dispositions sweeter,
Give him room. The cheater
Then snatches his fill, spilling
As much as he stuffs in his bill
And flies off alone. The others return
To feast together on ground and feeder
And I, through a glass dimly, learn,
Dear reader, about having one's way
And one's turn in good time.
Thats' what I have to say
In this rhyme.

NOV. 22, 2018

EVERYTHING IS BIGGER

Everything is bigger
Than little us can figger
Don't let it make you furious
Better to be curious!

I wrote this poem two weeks before the stroke — prophetic, indeed!

More mandalas made the week after the stroke, as I began to recover at home.

**JOURNAL ENTRY
(2 MONTHS POST STROKE)**

If a picture is worth a thousand words — and I've tried 'em all — perhaps this one best describes how I feel. The TPA drug saved me big time, but what remains is being on the outer edge of vertigo most of the time. It's like I'm pushing my way through pudding. With fatigue, it's worse, the pudding thickens, and I must carefully focus and be mindful as I make my way.

WE SPEND MOST DAYS*

My Zoey and me —
    In a rocking boat
        On a vertigo sea.
When waves affright
    We must sit tight
        But other days
Warm breezes play
    And ease our way.

But be what may,
        Calm seas or rough
This crew makes it through.
    This crew is tough!

*JOURNAL ENTRY...

...as I navigate my recovery from the stroke seven months ago, I'm still struggling with balance and coordination.

And this crew is tough! As the air cleared and I grew more accustomed to my condition, my thinking cleared as well.

MY CONVICTION

T'is my conviction
My stroke is but
A small affliction
Better yet a benediction
Filling heart and soul
With grace
Stilling mind
Slowing pace
Deepening being
Clearing seeing
I'm left awestruck
By this stroke of luck.

JOURNAL ILLUSTRATION — WINTER SOLSTICE, DECEMBER 21, 2018

I don't know where I read this little meme, but it worked for me:

> We do not think ourselves into a new way of living
> We live ourselves into a new way of thinking.

My late brother-in-law's "TINCTURE OF TIME" idea is what did it. The stroke gave me the time and leisure to live my way into a new, more relaxed, and acquiescent way of thinking and living and being. I had time to read, watch old movies, listen to music, journal, write poetry, and draw and draw and draw. No network TV. No TV news! (I had gone on an extended news fast when Trump got elected — I'm still on it!) I became a student at YouTube University, signed up for Audible books and became a regular Google consultant. The world's at our fingertips, folks, but the trick is to choose carefully.

JOURNAL ENTRY — JANUARY 2, 2019

Neurologists know
about how
my brain works

I only know
that it hurts — not pain
              but a strain

to be slightly off kilter

Up to the hilt
in a world that's a-tilt

Neurologists who know
Tell me *Be of good cheer*
You'll have your brain back

In six months to a year !

About this time — six months into my recovery — my beloved friend, Roz, broke her shoulder and I wrote her this poem as a get well card. She has recovered completely, as have I. Old friends — vintage wine.

THE NON-DEMISE OF TWO OLD GIRLFRIENDS

One, in her nineties, a shoulder she broke.
The other, age eighty, had a fortunate stroke
"People with fears think we've met our demise,"
(and the old cronies laugh until tears fill their eyes)
"Nonsense!" they insist, "We're kissed by our fate.
Despite the troubles, we celebrate. It's never too late.
It's never too late. It's never too late.
It's never too late. It's never too
Late. It's never too
late. It's never
too late!
Never
too
late.
Ne-
ver
too
late.
Ne-
ver
too
late.
Ne-
ver too
late. Never too late.

There are so many incredible, life-serving lessons that come along in elderhood(y) — too numerous to mention — or run the risk of writing like I know anything at all. I'll let my poems speak for me as I wind up this adventure of making the path by walking, making the book by writing, collecting memories, pondering and being everlastingly grateful for it all.

I DON'T KNOW

One morning out walking
I said *"I don't know"*
To a crow flying by
Who replied, *"It is so."*
Then by the path
a squirrel fluffed its tail,
Whom I greeted *"Hello.
I don't know,"*
but to no avail.
She gave only a sigh —
And I passed her by.
Then maples, oaks and sycamore
Raised their limbs in a mighty roar,
And chorused *"We don't know
We don't know
We don't know.
It is so!!"*
In counterpoint then
Chimed in a huge boulder
*I don't know either
And I'm a lot older!*
It was then I discovered
To walk in the flow
It is grace
To set pace
With *I don't know.*

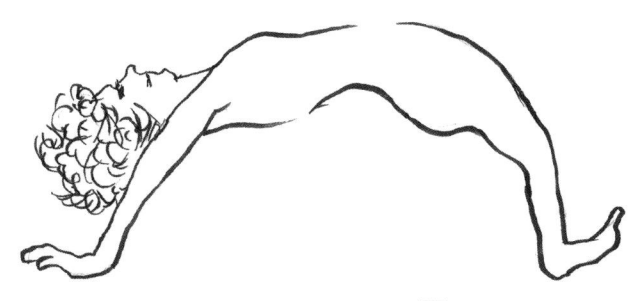

A Bridge

AGNOSTIC'S DEVOTION

I pray to *Beloved*.
The habit endures
Through most of my lifetime
Still, I'm not sure.
Who is the Listener?
Is there one at all?
Does an Allah
A Buddha
A Christ
Hear my call?
Or Gaia, The Mother?
Jehovah?
Or others?
And what of the Tao
Or the Wise Inner Me?
Could *Beloved*
Be all the above?
We'll see.

MEDITATION ON A BUMPER STICKER*

My karma ran over my dogma
Flattened it like a rug
Created resistance
To church and such
Caused me to shrug
And wonder how much
makes sense.
Meantime the rug
I mentioned before
Has morphed into magic —
Soaring and singing in the air
While far below crows and
stones and roses declare
There's more There's more
As breezes in birches
And sycamore trees
Whisper a chorus:
See! See!

*INSPIRED BY A BUMPER STICKER
DISCOVERED ONE DAY IN A PARKING LOT

FRACTALS OF GOD

We're fractals of God
Who gave us the nod
In a far distant past
When there came
A great blast
Providing thrust
And cosmic dust
To eventually be us.

Yes
Fractals of God
(Individuals, of course)
But all from the Source
Parts of a Whole
Bless my soul

A VERB

Life is a verb
Not a noun,
On the go
It is found —
In the flow
This I know!

I WEAR MY FAMILY LOOSE*

Like a sari, or a shift,
or colorful mu'u mu'u
(It's what I keep trying to do.)
With room to spare
To breathe the air
And heed with care
A need if there,
I've finally deduced
That I'm of better use
When I wear
my family loose.

*PS: truth to tell —
They wear me loose as well.

KEEP ME

Keep me

Alive while I'm still living

Keep me

Joy-full, Love-ing, Give-ing

Keep me

Aware and mindful and such

Keep me, Lord,

I love you this much!

ENLIGHTENMENT IS NOT

A spiritual spasm
A hip- hip hurrah
A sacred orgasm
A great aha

It is just
Recognition
Of my condition.
Enlightenment is not
A grand wham bam
It is only seeing
Who I Am

There's more G-O-D than ever in my life of late, albeit wrapped in a Cloud of Unknowing. Archbishop John Spong, in his late eighties, was quoted: "the older I get the more I believe and the fewer beliefs I have." Ditto.

LITANY

FREDERICK FRANCK WHEN ASKED —
DO YOU BELIEVE IN GOD?
RESPONDED — I BELIEVE IN NOTHING BUT GOD!

mothers
fathers
sisters
God
uncles and cousins
God and God
doctors nurses janitors God
neighbors gardeners
waitresses God
babies children teenagers
God
young adults elders middle-agers
mourners and praisers
protestors hell-raisers
God and God and God and God
stones and trees and mountains
God
dogs and cats and rabbits
God
earth animals all
God God God God
hearths and homes
prisons poems
God God God God
God God God
typhoons thunder lightening rain
God and God and God again
this litany will have no end
what I've missed
you add to the list

SOME GARDEN POEMS

LAUGHING FLOWERS

I spend time
In a garden of laughing flowers
Where air is so sweet
I could stay for hours.
I've given up churches
For under an arch
Of shaggy barked birches
I listen to leaves
Whisper gently to me
A simple, one-word homily:
See. See. See. See.

MEDITATION ON AN ELDERLY RHODODENDRON

My rhodie is old
But here's what I see
As her gnarly branches
Reach out to me:
Chartreuse shoots emerge
From every node
And tender green glows
In the dry undergrowth.
I suppose there's a lesson
Mother has for us here:
We're never too old
To grow newer each year.

EASTER

Her life takes a downward turn
in spring
while the garden grows.
Blinded by drama,
she misses the chartreuse shoots,
flutter of Phoenix wings
misses the metaphor entirely.
Engrossed in misery,
rightfully hers,
the garden grows
and pays her no mind
until she has time
to grow herself.

LAUGHTER IN THE GARDEN

The God Spirit laughs aloud in a garden —
In lavender, roses, clover, alyssum.
In prodigious anthills, profuse dandelions
And weeds of every persuasion.

God laughs aloud in proud oaks,
Maples, birches, sycamore —
In late arriving kousas,
Whose bright stars shine through the long days.

Spirit, Source, Ground of Being, Gaia, Mother —
Call it what you may — It laughs in summer.
In long, syrupy days of melting bones
And skin made rosy in the heat,

We laugh, too,
And delight in green outdoors —
So many shades of green
In the clear, warm air.

CARPE DIEM

Weeds seize the moment
They don't care
Will shimmy up
Your garden stair
Or fill a crack
And not look back
Then leave a million
Trillion seeds
We have a lot
To learn from weeds

EPIPHANY

The wondrousness
Beneath all things:
Seeds awakening
In spring;
Energy
Of butterfly wings
Felt across
The oceans wide;
And lunar swings
That pull the tide;
And systems
Deep inside of me
Managing impeccably.
I'm finally awakening
To wondrousness
In every thing.

RICHES

Clotty, black and thick as paste,
my garden soil is rich. I taste it
working there,
cultivating — giving air
to tender shoots,
pulling ancient ivy roots,
luxuriating in the earth —
a garden helps
you learn your worth.

SUNFLOWER

She leaps up
in a hurry of green.
I watch her progress
from seed to stalk
thick as an arm —
what a woman! Six feet tall
in two months' time —
her mighty flower-head lifts
in wonder, following the sun's arc.

But today she's depressed
neck bent, big moon face averted
staring at dirt. I hear her mutter
I've had my day, I've had my day
and want to shout *NO!*
Lift your head and
see the line of cardinals
wrens and finches
waiting to feast
on your seeds.

GOD

A purple finch —
Fringillidae —
Is nesting by
My patio door
Never before
Have I heard
From a bird
Songs more sweet
Than the tweets
He's emitting
Which is why
I stay sitting
And listening
To God —
Is that odd?

DRAWING BY CLOTILDE FARRELL

A gift comes to you through no action of your own,
free, having moved toward you without your beckoning...
You cannot earn it, or call it to you, or even deserve it.
And yet it appears... Gifts exist in a realm of humility and mystery —
as with random acts of kindness, we do not know their source.
—*BRAIDING SWEETGRASS* BY ROBIN WALL KIMMERER

THE GOD FROG

It came to me on a lovely spring day in May 2019. I was having lunch with my good friend, Roz, at a country restaurant, garden & gift shoppe. We had ordered our meals and were sitting at table in a light filled room, replete with huge windows, hanging plants, and displays of garden sculptures, pottery, and other gifts. Looking around, I spied a cement sculpture which positively called to me, so well it fit my quirky taste. It was a frog, meditating in lotus position. I picked up the thing, brought it back to our table, and peered at the price label beneath — $45.00. "I shouldn't — it's too much," said I, not quite able to justify the cost to myself, and placed the piece back on the display shelf.

Our sandwiches arrived and shortly afterwards, as we're munching and chatting, the waitress reappeared with a gift bag and placed it before me. "Someone would like you to have this," said she. Huh? What? How come? — and I open it to find the frog. The "someone" wanted to and has remained anonymous, — a random act of kindness which, to this day has charmed my heart and left me awestruck. (The God Frog is holding court now, as I write this while looking out on my tiny patio garden.) I believe I know who the gift-giver was, a lone diner who was sitting nearby, although I never met him to thank him in person. But I spent hours that afternoon, making a card with poem — hoping the vibrations of love and gratitude which I felt would reach him anyway. I later delivered the card to the restaurant with the instructions to give it to the kind young man, if he came in again.

To the young man, a stranger

In a red and black shirt,

Who dined in this country café:

Namaste, I say,

And greet in you

The god

Who gave me

The frog —

So gratuitous and kind —

(the likes I've experienced never)

You have blown my mind!!!

It will grace my garden forever!

THANK YOU

SAVOR THE MOMENT

Savor

The moment

Be aware

You're aware

Ingest

The air

Breathe in

Breath out

Don't care

What it's about

Let it all be

And see

See

!

Lift up the self by the Self

and don't let the self droop low

For the Self is the self's only friend

and the self is the Self's only foe.

BHAGAVAD GITA, CH 6 V5

NEW YEAR'S DAY POEM*

I'm not psychic or prescient
I can't see what's ahead
Nostradamus' predictions
Fill me with dread
As tv prattles on
Its tidings of doom
I'm likely to take myself
Out of the room
And newspaper headlines
Give me such starts
I quickly must turn
To the section on Arts.
So am I in a bubble
Is my head in the sand?
Or have I honed skills
For survival — a stand
To be taken at seventy-one
When I waken each morning
And choose to have fun —
To set coffee brewing
Breathe in the good air
Eliminate stewing
On matters out there
I'm unable to scratch
A dent in at all. My patch
Of the planet's defenseless
And small — but friendly and kind,
I make it that way,
And that's what I find
Myself thinking today.

* I WROTE THIS IN 2008 — IT'S JUST AS RELEVANT TODAY

A PRAYER PORTRAIT

... whatever it means ... whatever prayer is. I take it to mean sending energy — I call it "grammergy" — I call it "heart sparks." Nowhere do I find this more so than when I am drawing — particularly when I'm drawing a portrait. I can't help but try to climb into the being of my subject — his or her "I AM." Mary Oliver refers to a poem without feeling (or empathy) as a report. Certainly, this holds true even more so with a portrait. Drawing a portrait is a prayer for my subject — even if it's a stranger from a photograph. Somehow, the BIG LOVE takes in my tiny efforts and my creative energy reaches out and connects with my subject. I call this MAGIC!! I call this portrait ABUELA — Spanish for grandmother. My nephew, Steve, took the photo in Mexico on the Day of the Dead. She is Everywoman to me — every grandmother. She is me.

BYE-BYE, JEAN

CREATED JANUARY 12, 2022, THE DAY JEAN DIED

My dear friend, Jean, died last winter. Jean, Martha and Joyce, my other dearest friend, formed a friendship triad that has been a source of mutual love, support, and delight for many years. Jean is the first of my best friends to pass — a trailblazer. But, as I gaze into the Cloud of Unknowing, I have no ideas this about particular trail. Jean was 85, I'm 84 and Joyce will be 90 in a few months. We'll find out soon enough but meantime, life remains full and satisfying right where I am. There's still art to make, friends and family with whom to spend time, books to read, portraits to draw, journals to fill, poems to write ...

In Florida together — February 2020

RANDOM THOUGHTS ON A DEFINITION OF LOVE

non-possessive delight in
the particularity of the other

Non-possessive comes first
It's not about me
Or I-ing or My-ing —
It's about delight.
Possessiveness strangles
playful and fragile delight.
Delight dances in particularities —
Thirteen billion human particularities
On our planet — no two thumbprints alike —
or snowflakes. Particularities need not be human.
Start with flowers: tulips, roses, lilies, phlox.
irises, daisies, lilacs, sweet alyssum, mums ...

PAINTING BY LENNY MOSKOWITZ

HERE AND NOW

I move in a space
Quite close to my face —
A place called HERE.
It's clear I'll be HERE
For the rest of my days
So don't ask me ways
To get out of HERE
Or how
Or to where or when
Because NOW
Is when
As ever it's been
And wherever you go
You are HERE.

JOURNAL ENTRY — SEPTEMBER 18, 2020

Glory be to God — it IS a wonderful life! Joy and delight spills over me in waves. Waves which seem to spill over my family and friends on these pages. And the garden is spilling over as well. I took this pic of it while walking Zoey (her name means LIFE in Greek!) and thinking about autumn — TODAY IS ROSHASHONA — it's the Jewish new year and my new year — my 82nd birthday is next week. Perhaps I'll get a new poem for the occasion, but this one still works perfectly well:

BIRTHDAY POEM

My patch of the planet is small, with no title

my role in events, miniscule but vital:

... a grain of salt ... a drop of wine ... a twilight glimmer

... this light of mine. I let it shimmer and let it shine.

I wrote the poem three years ago and it still holds. I get to let my life shimmer and shine. I get to spend hours just thinking about stuff, just being, listening a lot to Richard Rohr, Rupert Spira and many other teachers who help me. I have time (tincture of time!) to create stuff of no particular value (except to me), like HOPE flags, birthday cards, journal entries replete with pics and poems and whatever else inspires me. I get to make portraits and give them away — like the portraits in memory of Sarah Williams and Jack the dog and all the drawings and poems given away during sheltering in this winter. The other day Joyce and I spent several hours on facetime as she did a tarot reading for me. It was very interesting and indicated quite positively that it's time now to put more energy into A BRIDGE NOT A WALL. All is in readiness. I must step more agressively into the adventure of creating this book!

It is, indeed, a wonderful life. I avoid watching the news — but pray continuously for help and grace and enlightenment for our crazy, mixed-up country and world. Enough said.

EIGHTIETH BIRTHDAY PRAYER

As long as you want me around,
Lord, I'll stay.
But help me keep my marbles clear,
Know my elbow from my rear,
Have my friends and loved ones near,
This I pray to you today;
As long as you want me around,
Lord, I'll stay.

JOURNAL ENTRY — JULY 13, 2022

I did it.

POSTSCRIPT

As I wrap up this BRIDGE NOT A WALL, I can't help but feel conflicted. Mary Oliver, my favorite poet, felt the same way:

> I am so distant from the hope of myself
> In which I have goodness, and discernment,
> And never hurry through the world
> But walk slowly and bow often.

... a tall order, that hope, and a steep bridge. It's taking a lifetime to get over myself.

Mercifully, I am surrounded by loving and patient people — family and friends who help me make my way, for whom I am everlastingly grateful. A sign hangs over my door, gift from one of those friends, which reads IT'S A WONDERFUL LIFE — and it is: wonder-full, terrifying, hilarious, messy, fun, impossible, glorious — and not over yet.

The Beginning

A LIST OF INFLUENCERS

In no particular order and by no means complete.

Dalai Lama	Ralph Waldo Emerson	Brene Brown
Richard Rohr	Byron Katie	Elaine Pagels
Rupert Spira	William Stafford	Ken Wilbur
Matthew Fox	Ted Kooser	Lao Tzu
Yungi Mingur Rinpoche	Teillard de Chardin	Dag Hammarskjold
Yogananda Paramahansa	Lucille Clifford	Rabbi Zalman Schachter-Shalomi
Baba Ram Das	Naomi Shihad Nye	
Marcus Borg	Robert Frost	Betty Friedan
Dominick Crossan	Meister Eckhart	Gloria Steinem
Miguel Ruiz	Carl Jung	Pema Chodron
Eckhart Tolle	Judith Viorst	Deepak Chopra
Eknath Eswaren	C.S. Lewis	David Hawkins
Anthony de Mello	J.R.R. Tolkien	Martin Buber
Cynthia Bourgeault	Madeleine L'Engle	Paul Tillich
Alice Miller	Gary Wills	Robert Frost
Alice Walker	Eli Weisel	Billy Collins
Emily Dickinson	Thich Nat Hanh	Alice Walker
e e cummings	Sogyal Rinpoche	Robin Wall Kimmerer
Henry David Thoreau	Anne Lamott	Krista Tippit

ACKNOWLEDGEMENTS

My gratitude is measureless, my thankyous innumerable

First and foremost, to my beloved six children: Kerry, Stephen, Mark, John, Sarah and Julie — you have shaped and made me, we have grown up and continue to grow up together. You've encouraged me in this Bridge adventure and laugh with me as I wind my way through elderhood. I am grateful to you individually and collectively beyond words… and to the children of my children — thank you for the privilege of having you in my life. I've gotten to be Mama, Grammy, and now Gigi (Great Grandmother) — a priceless fortune, an invaluable treasure.

To Stephen, who back during early COVID sequestering when I was sending out a poem de jour to the whole family, asked for and is underwriting the publication of A BRIDGE, encouraging and urging me on throughout the two plus year project. Thank you and thank you again.

Susan, my friend, coach and yay-sayer, has lovingly pushed and pulled, carrot and sticked me every step of the way. Without our weekly Monday morning 9AM phone conversations I would never have gotten to "I did it."

Pam, with two marvelous books of poetry to her credit and another on the way, is my beloved niece, friend, editor, and advisor par excellence. She has continually assured me I DO NOT have to insert "Yikes!" asides in my text and suggested I keep my exclamation points to a minimum. I love this woman — exclamation points required here!!!

Finally, to Suzanne, our newest and treasured family member — a graphic artist and book designer — who stepped up and offered her services in the laying out and making pretty this hodgepodge collection of my bits and pieces — a necessary artform indeed, for which I'm very grateful.

Years ago, I learned a mantra suggested by a Hindu wise woman who lived in Stamford, Connecticut — I never met her — just read about her in the newspaper. People from near and far sought her counsel. Her mantra, offered to one and all, was just this:

Thank you for everything
I have no complaints whatsoever

I've been saying it ever since.

IN MEMORIUM

Sarah Williams

Jack the Dog